WAKE UP CALL™

An inspiring collaboration
of life changing stories

Joe Trimboli

YOUR WAKE-UP CALL
An inspiring collaboration of life changing stories.
Joe Trimboli

www.joetrimboli.com

1st Edition. 1st printing 2022

Cover Concept Design and Interior Design:
Steve Walters, Oxygen Publishing Inc.

Editor: Richard Tardif

Independently Published by
Oxygen Publishing Inc.
Montreal, QC, Canada
www.oxygenpublishing.com

ISBN: 978-1-990093-64-7
Imprint: Independently published

Dedication

This book is dedicated to you, the reader. The one who chooses to wake up and be the change you want to see in the world. You, who trade in time spent doing something easier, for time invested in doing something a little more uncomfortable. For taking action toward becoming the person you need to become, in order to begin living the life you want to live.

As you get better, everything in your life gets better!

"I can do nothing for you but work on myself,
you can do nothing for me but work on yourself!"

– Ram Dass

Joe Trimboli

Table of Contents

Your Wake Up Call

Foreword

By Brian Proctor

You may not know it yet, but you have this book in your hands for a reason.

My father, Bob Proctor has always said, "We are either growing, or we're dying—It is up to us." He meant that we are either learning and moving forward or playing it safe and not stepping into our greatness.

This book is your inspiration for stepping into your greatness!

I found myself completely drawn into the stories shared on these pages, but what struck me the most, was how vulnerable the messages were. You will "feel" the emotion with which each author shared their stories and insights, and you will come away with a new awareness. I know that a few stories here will touch you in a way you did not expect. When that happens, you may change or question your beliefs in a way that will cause you to gain a new understanding of how you can live a better life—a more purposeful life. Not only for yourself, but you will see how you can also inspire those close to you.

I have always been a morning person, so when Joe Trimboli asked me to come on one of his Wake Up Calls as a guest at 5 a.m., it was an easy yes for two reasons. First, I have incredible respect for what Joe is doing and how he is helping people, just like you, wake up to a better life.

The second reason was that he wanted me to share some of the lessons that I learned from my father. Sharing those lessons has always been an honour, and watching how those lessons are received has always brought me an incredible amount of "psychic income." I know how fortunate I am to have Bob Proctor as my father; sharing what I have learned from him with others feels like my duty and a way to honour his legacy.

The call we did together was wonderful. What struck me the most when reading this book, was that several of the stories you will find here, were written by some of the people that were on that same call. Seeing their faces and watching how they all took part in sharing and supporting one another was really something special to see. They are a remarkable group so it is only fitting that the stories they have to share are something special.

I have known Joe for a few years now. He has a community of people who, through their stories, have found a way to heal, motivate, and help each other live a better life. This book is a result of that.

I know you will benefit from a special feature that Joe calls "Pep Talks." After each story, he sums up the lesson and gives you the tools to implement that lesson right where you are.

Some stories will shock you, and some will surprise you. Some will wrap you in a warm blanket, and some will heal your heart. Each one has a valuable lesson to draw from. All it takes is for just one of these stories to resonate with you and guide you to the person you have always known you are.

As you read this book, you will become more aware that you are worthy of the good you desire and seek, and that everything you need is already within you.

There is something that I have heard Joe say many times and also read in several of the stories. "What you don't fix, your kids inherit." I love that statement. No matter where you are in life, you will resonate and learn from the messages you will find throughout this book.

My hope is that you enjoy and learn from some of the stories as much as I have.

Brian Proctor

Preface

"Tell me what you want, and I'll show you how to get it!"

How could Bob Proctor make such a promise? In the past, I'd have shut down everything that followed, and written the speaker off as another guru making promises that were true, maybe for everyone else, but not for me. This time I listened, and what followed was so good that I quickly became obsessed with what I was hearing.

Someone turned the lights on, and I could see for the first time. I couldn't wait to learn more. This information was so simple but incredibly powerful that my life began making sense. For the first time I could see the cause of my so-called "bad luck."

As time went on and I studied more, I discovered that there is no need for us to struggle the way we do. We don't have to remain the victims of the circumstances and conditions in our lives. This information was so good that I couldn't help but want to share it with anyone who would listen. I shared every chance I got. If someone complained to me about their day, job, finances, etc., I'd offer a different perspective, and I could feel their energy shift almost immediately. Their day would unfold differently. They'd take action different from how they would typically act, and later tell me how much it helped and how they achieved a different result than they usually would. Funny, all it took was a different perspective. Different thinking. A different energy.

I decided to invite three of my friends to read and study with me on the phone on weekday mornings, and they too quickly began seeing improvements in their lives. We continued our calls, and the more we studied the more convinced we were that this information could help anyone.

People would hear about our call and ask if they could join us. For a long time I'd refuse, not wanting to change the dynamic of our group. We had a good thing going. The four of us would read to understand the book, not just to finish it. We would speak openly and share things people wouldn't typically share. I didn't want to compromise that.

But eventually the universe would have its way, and I'd find myself with over a thousand members, all who came by word of mouth, inspired by friends, family or from social media posts of people passionately sharing how the call was helping them. People from all walks of life who, in some serendipitous way, found themselves right at home in a community of like-minded individuals, all looking to become better versions of themselves. Some are looking for a change. Some are looking to figure out what they want—some with big goals and some without goals. Everyone joined for different reasons, but all came away with a better sense of who they are, what they're capable of, and the peace of mind that comes with a greater understanding that supports a better quality of thinking, and ultimately, a better quality of life.

One of the big lessons I learned, and one that you'll hear about in some of the stories in this collection, is to not let "the how" stop you from deciding what you want. I could not have told you then how I'd end up "sharing this information with people all over the world," but looking back I can now tell you how it all unfolded. That's a story for another time, but let's just say this, you don't get what you want; you get what you're in harmony with.

What these authors learned to do was think. If you want a new result, you need new thoughts. Einstein said, "We can't solve problems by using the same thinking we used when we created them." We spend too little time understanding the advice that the greatest thinkers have left us with. All knowledge has been here since the beginning of time, but we're all too busy being entertained by other people's thinking to do any of our own—we'd rather be entertained than study. What I can tell you is that studying is the key. It's not the studying we did in school where we were taught what to think. It's the type of studying that will teach us how to think. People study for years to become masters in their professions. Doctors and lawyers study for seven to ten years. Tradespeople log thousands of hours working alongside their superiors in apprenticeships. We possess the most powerful thing in the universe, the mind, and we spend zero to little time understanding how to use its power. We should study life, ourselves and the laws of our beings, like surgeons study before ever being allowed to perform surgery. Learn how to think and how to get in harmony with the laws of the universe. That's how you tap into your unlimited potential as a human being.

I now understand how Bob could have made that promise! It's a promise you make when you know that EVERYTHING happens by law. Goal setting is an intellectual exercise, and goal achieving is a lawful process. Now, I too can say, "Tell me what you want, and I'll show you how to get it."

As you read these stories, that light you have within will shine a little brighter. You'll see something you didn't see before. You'll catch a glimpse of what's possible for you, but more than anything, you'll come to understand and know that you are 100% responsible for the results in your life. Stop letting your results control you—you can be in control of your results.

Introduction

In this book, you'll find a collaboration of stories from everyday people of all ages, from students and stay-at-home moms to lawyers and entrepreneurs. They have all inspired me with their personal growth.

I don't care where you're at in life. I don't care about your financial status. I'm not interested in what you do for a living or how you earn your money. It makes no difference how old you are, and it doesn't matter if or where you went to school, where you've been or how you got there.

What I do care about is:

What do you want? What is your goal? What image do you hold in your mind for where you're going? Few people ever spend enough time building or putting energy into their goal. We can create an image in our mind using the most powerful force in the universe—our imagination. We can then use another powerful force, our will, to focus on that image so that it gets the energy it needs to move into physical form.

In every story, you will find that with each transformation the author already possessed everything they needed to make the shift toward the life they wanted. You too have everything you need to begin at once to start creating the life you've imagined.

I invite you to look at all areas of your life and ask, "What do I really want?"

What do I really want?

It was a question that seemed impossible for me to answer for a time. My beliefs were so distorted that I couldn't permit myself to want anything. My conditions and circumstances made it impossible for me to see past what already existed in my life.

"What do you really want? More money? A better, more fulfilling job? A healthy relationship? Peace of mind? To be a better parent? Write a book maybe?"

I'm pressing you here because you may have bought into the idea that we should be happy with what we've got. That wanting more is greedy. "This is just the way it is. You shouldn't be too picky—you should be realistic," but the truth is, it's our nature to want more. We should always be grateful, but never satisfied. We should always be striving for more. We're either growing or dying—but we're never standing still. Being grateful and wanting more is not a contradiction.

We are not our name, our physical body, or our job title. We are spiritual beings. We are a mass of energy. We have unlimited potential and the most inner part of us knows this, but we can never go beyond where we think we can go. We are built to want to do more, be more, and have more. That's why runners want to run faster; jumpers wish to jump higher; salespeople desire more sales. The trouble is, we limit this limitless part of who we are by our limited thinking. This unexpressed desire causes frustration in our soul—at the core of who we truly are.

Who you truly are

You don't know yourself well enough to know you can have whatever you want. You don't know that there are laws that govern everything in the universe, and that everything happens by law. You don't see yourself as a creator who can take the invisible and move it into its physical form. You don't know that you have been programmed to think and behave the way you do, and that habitual behaviour is largely responsible for your results.

We've been treating symptoms and not causes. We lack awareness. There are things we know that we know (I know that two plus two equals four). There are things we know that we don't know (I know I don't know how to perform open-heart surgery). But then there are things that we don't know that we don't know. Here is where we find the root of all problems.

My Wake Up Call

One day while listening to my mentor, self-help author and lecturer, Bob Proctor, I had my wake up call.

I heard, "What you don't fix, your kids inherit!"

Those words may as well have been a fury of punches to the gut. I was 40 years old, a father to three beautiful girls—Sofia, ten, and my twins, Ava and Erica, seven. My girls are the most important things in my life. I was a jaded man working hard, frustrated, struggling, and constantly worrying whether I could support them and give them the life they deserve. I was angry! Why was I put on this earth to struggle like this? It's not like I didn't have justification for feeling this way.

I had cancer when I was 21, bankrupt by 33, and at 40 still under a mountain of debt. I felt completely unfulfilled in my work and looking to get into something else, while being the only income provider in my household. "Stuck? Ummm ya!"

These girls didn't ask to be born! Rita, my wife, and I brought them into this world. They blessed our lives with riches we could never have dreamt. I owed them a secure, healthy, happy life.

Your Wake Up Call is not a book where you will read about all the lessons I learned or shared with the authors, (that one is on its way) but where you will find the inspiration in knowing that you already have everything you need to achieve anything you desire. You just need to become aware of the things you don't know that you don't know and raise your level of awareness. I'll admit that the last sentence was meaningless when I first heard it, but I kept studying and now understand its magnitude.

"One reason people succeed is that they have knowledge other people don't." — Tony Robbins.

Your transformation does not have to be complicated or laborious. You don't have to rearrange the stars in the universe, but you will have to learn the rules to this game of life. Your transformation can begin when you become aware of something that causes you to question a belief or see something you didn't know was already there. As Dr. Wayne Dyer said, "Change the way you look at a thing, and the thing you're looking at changes." You will learn that there are Truths, and there are appearances. We've come to live by the appearance of things. The secret is to live by the image we create in our mind for what we want, and learn to live by these Truths so we can continue to focus on that image, instead of our current results.

Universal Laws

Nikola Tesla said, "If you want to find the secrets of the universe, think in terms of energy, frequency and vibration."

Everything in this Universe is energy and everything vibrates—nothing rests. "Everything" includes the book you're holding, the chair you're sitting in, the highlighter and the pen you might be using to make notes, and YOU! You are a mass of energy, and you are vibrating on a frequency. The thoughts you think and internalize cause your feelings. Those feelings are the vibration you're in—good vibes/bad vibes. Whatever you're feeling is always expressed through the body in terms of your actions. Your actions get your results. The vibration determines the frequency you're on and that determines what you can receive. You can only receive whatever is on the frequency you're vibrating on. There is a connection between your thoughts, feelings, actions and results.

You have a conscious and a subconscious mind. The conscious mind is the intellectual mind. It's where you have the ability to choose your thoughts. You can accept or reject any idea. It's where the higher mental faculties reside. These faculties are: perception, reason, memory, the will, imagination and intuition. The way you use these faculties is dependent upon your paradigm—your current programming. What were you brought up to believe? Money is the root of all evil? More money, more problems? Money is for other people? There's a limited supply? People will screw you? You have to be smart to be successful? What's right? What's wrong? What you should and shouldn't do? What you're capable of and what you're not? You didn't choose your beliefs—you accepted them. You're shy? You're stupid? Whatever you believe will determine how you use your faculties: how you perceive things, what you remember, how you reason, how you use your imagination, and what you focus on.

Your subconscious mind is the emotional mind. It's where your feelings are. Feeling is the vibration. Your subconscious mind has no ability to reject, it can only accept whatever you impress upon it. It has no ability to determine what's real or what's imagined. This is where the paradigm resides. The operating system when you're on autopilot.

It is said that your conscious mind is male, and your subconscious mind is female. It's also been said that your subconscious mind is like the earth, it will return to you whatever you plant in it. Your conscious mind is where you choose the seeds to be planted.

The paradigm has almost exclusive control of your habitual behaviour, and almost all your behaviour is habitual. The experts tell us that we're operating from the subconscious mind 95% of the time. That means, you're only thinking on purpose 5% of the time. What's in control of your thinking? What is your automatic reaction to things? Most people can't think beyond their emotions. They are stuck because the program stays in control of how they use their mental faculties, thereby preventing any "right" thinking. You didn't choose this programming; it was installed by other people, past experiences, social media, the news, and other outside forces. If we're going to change our results, we have to change the program. The only way to install the new program is by the same method you received the one you currently have—repetition! Everything that's easy for you is because you have a program to support it. The language you speak, driving a car, and brushing your teeth; they all started by giving conscious thought to what you were doing until you repeated it enough times where you came to a point that you can do it without thinking.

Toxic positivity

If we're going to be successful, we'll need to develop faith based on understanding to support our new way of thinking. A deep understanding that will support the "right" thinking that will eventually change the way you habitually think. This is not to suggest you reject your emotions. You must allow yourself to feel what you are feeling, without judgement or guilt! You're human and will have very human emotions. People will say things like, "look on the bright side," or "be grateful, it could be worse," but they really don't understand what they're saying and probably choose the wrong time to offer this encouragement. There are laws that provide a change of perception and expectation. The Law of Rhythm states that everything is cyclical. There are changing seasons as there are changing phases in our lives. Good times will follow bad times and vice versa. Nothing stays the same. There's also the Law of Polarity, everything has an equal and opposite. Things that appear to be opposites are actually two inseparable parts of the same thing. That means that if something is bad, there has to be good in it too. Knowing that these things are a matter of law moves us from surface level positivity, to a change in mindset based on a deep understanding of how things actually work. Developing a deep understanding when things are going well, that will support your thinking when things go south, is a good idea. A boxer doesn't train for a fight while he's fighting for the belt. He builds his stamina and skill when he's not constantly being punched. Being constantly exposed to the right information provides some of the repetition necessary to change the programming. The right information will support the right thinking which will support you in changing your frequency when you're ready to move past your emotions. A positive mindset doesn't mean you ignore your feelings or force yourself to think positively. It's a mindset built upon Truth and understanding you can use to shift your focus from where you're at to where you want to be.

You reap what you sow

There are many laws we need to understand and obey. Some of the stories and pep talks make mention of these laws, but not all are discussed in this book. Some laws are mentioned repeatedly aiming to offer different examples of their application. These laws influence how energy, frequencies and vibrations work. No one is immune to their effects. You will suffer the consequences of violating these laws, regardless of whether you are aware of them or not. How do we obey or work in harmony with these laws if we don't even know what they are? We're playing the game of life without knowing the rules. Will something fall "up" for a person who doesn't know about the Law of Gravity? In like manner, our ignorance of any one of these laws will not spare us from their consequences. You cannot plant tomato seeds and expect to get strawberries just because you want strawberries. You cannot tune into an AM frequency and expect to hear an FM broadcast. You can't put out bad and expect to get good just because you want good. You don't get what you want; you get what you're in harmony with.

We must also understand that the laws work perfectly for every person, every time and they don't discriminate. We wonder why bad things happen to good people. If Mother Teresa fell off a twenty-story building, would she be spared because she did so much good in the world? If you aren't obeying these laws, you will suffer the consequences—period! These laws, which are as real as the Law of Physics, dictate "the rules to the Game of Life" and make it possible to create the life we want.

Known effects of unknown causes

I discovered that because we don't know the laws of the universe, we're forced to make things up to explain the effects of unknown causes—our results.

For example, I used to think I was unlucky. I used to say that, "If there was no such thing as bad luck, I'd have no luck at all." I believed that I just couldn't catch a break no matter what I did. And the worst part was that I would keep telling people how unlucky I was.

Those were all lies. The truth was that I wasn't working in harmony with some of the laws. For one, the Law of Cause and Effect—what you put out, you get back. If you've ever played with Newton's cradle or seen one in action, you see that if you swing three balls, you get three balls in return. You never swing three balls and only affect the two remaining balls. That is the Truth. "I'm unlucky" is the lie that explained my results when I didn't understand I was violating the Law of Cause and Effect. To add insult to injury, I'd keep talking about what I didn't want! I kept giving attention to what I didn't want to happen in my life, which was a violation of another law, the Perpetual Transmutation of Energy. Energy is always moving into form. Well, thought is energy! EVERYTHING is energy! Remember?

American philosopher Ralph Waldo Emerson once said, "The only thing that can grow is the thing you give energy to."

So, not only was I ignorant of the Law of Cause and Effect, I kept justifying and explaining my results in the only way I knew how—to complain about them and without realizing it, was giving energy to what I didn't want.

I also wasn't aware that I was operating on a frequency that didn't have what I wanted so "no matter what I do, nothing works out." Another violation! The Law of Vibration and Attraction! Imagine what happens to the self-image! "I'm not good enough." "I don't know enough." "I'm not smart enough." "What's the point of trying?" Think of how this person will operate. You will never outperform your self-image! The saddest part is the fact that everyone is fully capable; they are just unaware. It doesn't matter how hard you try, if you're not in harmonious vibration with the result you want, you cannot have that result—and that's according to law!

What are you giving energy to?

Put the book down for just a minute and think. What have you been giving energy to? What have you been worrying about? What are you expecting? Have you been focused on building wealth, or are you worried about debt? Are you focused on your health, or are you worrying about sickness? Are you focusing on peace and harmony or complaining about all the lunatics in your life? Do you say you want world peace but then swear at the first driver that cuts you off? Life doesn't have to be a struggle.

What if you didn't think about what you didn't want? What if you begin to give energy only to what you do want? What could that mean in your life?

If you're stuck, I learned that you're focusing on what already is (the debt, the medical report, the unproductive employees, the messy house). To get unstuck, focus on what you want and take immediate action.

Nothing happens without a decision

How many times have you not acted on an opportunity because of your current conditions and circumstances? When an opportunity comes, we say things like, "I don't have the money," or "I don't have the time," or "I don't know enough." Decisions should have little to do with the present. We're already here. If you want new results, start with a new decision. Decisions are made to take you where you want to go, to get you thinking on the frequency that has the goal. They are made to bring something new. Break out of your habitual way of thinking and take control of your higher mental faculties, to think what you want to think instead of what you've been programmed to think.

The trouble is, we get stuck on "the how." We look around and don't see any of the resources we're going to need to achieve our goal, or how these things will show up in the future. We try to figure out how we're going to do it, and because we can't, we never make the decision—we never set the goal. Nothing changes. Eventually you feel like there's nothing you want. You have no more passion for things. You dismiss the idea of what you want before you can even want it because you can't see how it's going to happen.

"The How"

Don't let "the how" stop you from setting the goal. Once you make the decision, then you can start asking "what are some things I can do to move me toward my goal?" As you begin taking action, everything you need will show up when you need it. Where there is no demand, there will be no evidence of supply. When a demand is created, the supply will show up.

Edison didn't know how he was going to get the light bulb to shine, until he did. The Wright brothers didn't know how they would get that bicycle off the ground, until they did. Edmund Hillary didn't know how he was going to get to the top of Mount Everest, until he got to the top of that mountain.

Don't let the big names cause you to believe that they had something you don't. We all have genius locked up inside us. The process is the same for everyone and we use big names because we are familiar with their stories. You probably don't know my Uncle Nick or my friend Dan, so I don't use their stories. Consider that these were ordinary people until they figured out how to do what they did. Edison was still an ordinary inventor on the nine-hundred-and-ninety-ninth failed attempt to turn the light on. It wasn't until the one-thousandth that he became, who we now know as Thomas Edison.

Start where you are with what you have. You won't be able to see steps seventy-eight and seventy-nine, but you can probably see your next two or three steps. Take those. When you've completed those steps, the next ones you need to take will show up.

A key part of this lesson is that the purpose of a goal is to cause you to grow. You aren't the person that is capable of achieving your goal today. You must grow into that person. As you're figuring out how to do it, you're becoming qualified. You will make mistakes and will learn from them. You will learn to respond and not react. You will notice how important it is to maintain the right attitude, no matter what is going on outside of you. You will discover what works and what doesn't. If you become ungrateful, stressed out, or begin complaining about the difficulties you're encountering, you will find that the universe will not bless you with more until you can prove you can handle what you've already got.

When the student is ready

Your Wake Up Call can come at any point. There is a saying, alternately attributed to Buddha Siddhartha Guatama Shakyamuni and the

Theosophists, that goes, "When the student is ready, the teacher will appear." I hope and wish you find what you need in the pages of this book. Like you, the people behind these stories had been where you are when they had their Wake Up Call. If you doubt yourself, you should know right here and now, "God does not call the qualified. He qualifies the called." So, start where you are with what you have and know that you will grow into the person you need to become to have what you desire.

You'll find evidence of this in every movie you watch, every book and story you read. As author Donald Miller writes in his 2022 book *Hero on a Mission: A path to a meaningful life,* it's the hero's journey. The hero is the underdog at the beginning of the story. They are the weakling, the geek, and the narcissist. Then they're given some adversity, a challenge, or a villain to conquer. They meet a guide who teaches them how to draw out their dormant superpower. The soon-to-be hero grows into a person capable of overcoming challenges. They become the hero who triumphs over the villain.

May Your Wake Up Call and the shared vulnerability of its contributors, be your guide to the transformation that will have you claiming victory over any adversities in your life.

Vibrate higher my friends.

Pep Talks

My name is Joe. My friends call me Pep. It's an Italian thing. It comes from my given name Giuseppe that gets shortened to Peppe, which is shortened further to Pep.

At the end of each author's story, I've added a little commentary, affectionately known in our calls as "Pep Talks." My goal is to highlight the main lessons or takeaways in each story. Although each story likely has dozens of ground-breaking lessons, I have kept the commentary short and sweet, and addressed only one or two lessons from each author's contribution, in the hope that you will relate it to whatever is going on in your life.

Pep Talk

Each Pep Talk will get you to see how all these transformations are rooted in certain laws or principles that apply to everyone, and connect the dots between the author's story and our everyday lives. Be sure to take a minute to stop and think how you can apply these lessons to any area of your life where you may be struggling.

I knew something wasn't right. My doctors told me my intermittent bleeding likely stemmed from my body going into menopause. I had just turned 50. The Smear test told a different story. There was too much bleeding to be a coincidence, and the fact they couldn't get an accurate look at my cervix said something bigger was at play.

Enter Carl the Cervical Alien

I heard the dreaded words on September 29th when I had my consultation with the gynecologist at St. John's Hospital in West Lothian, Scotland. That day, I would go by myself, convinced the abnormality was only a polyp, easily dealt with through a simple medical procedure. I would be in and out, wham, bam, and thank you ma'am. My best friend, Kirsty, insisted that she come with me. I am as thankful to her as I am to Tracy.

It wasn't a polyp. The gynecologist confirmed her suspicions: cervical cancer. Two biopsies, bloodwork, and a plethora of scans, CT, MRI, PET, and officially: Stage 3 Cervical cancer with a 2.5-inch growth on my cervical gland and two cancerous spots in my pelvic lymph nodes.

I cried that day and the following month while I came to grips with my diagnosis and the coming treatments. I thought I would die because Tracy did, and I didn't know anyone who went through cancer treatment without dying. It would not be the end for me, I promised. I had so much to accomplish. My dreams were limitless.

Crafting a Superhero mindset

I knew my glass-half-empty thinking would not get me the results I wanted. I had to act differently, and the first step was to change my thoughts, a tool I learned in the Wake Up Call. Thought powers everything! How I speak to myself, sometimes on a subconscious level, was negative and had to change as well. I had to look at any goal, big or small, beginning at the end result and how I would feel about achieving that goal.

I started with gratitude—for my life, what I had accomplished, and what was ahead. I wrote out my gratitudes every day, and I committed to writing gratitudes for one year. The gratitude could be as simple as waking up, the love of my soul dog, Kao, and the goals I've achieved. It was simple and consistent. It fuelled my day and every activity.

Looking at the results from the end goal had an impact. I started imagining my cancer journey not as a dire situation but as a success, one that had me ringing the cancer bell, eradicating the tumour, and developing a healthy body, mind, and spirit. I committed to every minute, hour, and day, which was damned hard, especially when the scans painted a different picture.

I felt dirty, scared, and unworthy—a paradigm that had followed me from my previous life's chapter. Like Carl the Cervical Tumour, it had to go. It had no place in my life—it was up to me to change. My Gratitude 365+ practice was the beginning. Affirmations followed, along with my daily Reiki practices.

Over a month, I received five chemo sessions, 25 external radiations and three internal radiations. It was intense, scary, yet empowering.

More than my diagnosis

Friends, family, and neighbours offered support and a shoulder when needed. My Wake Up Call friends reached out—they knew about my mindset journey. I had so many people offering what they could: from rides to the hospital to visits and gifts to remind me I was more than my cancer diagnosis.

I had my next lightbulb moment outside the Edinburgh Cancer Centre following my fifth and final chemo treatment. Despite the current health crisis, I had never been as happy with myself and my life as I was at that moment. Because of my journey, I was grateful, happy, and inspired to help others.

At every appointment, I delivered Reiki to my tumour, tapping into Source (Universe, God) and sending healing to my entire body, willing Carl's demise and visualizing him breaking away and evaporating from my body. I bought my bell and bells for others to ring, knowing my efforts would be successful and cause the death of Carl. Wearing my Wonder Woman socks, I danced into my radiation appointments. I didn't give up as I would have in the past—I didn't expect the other shoe to drop. There was no shoe! There was me, my mind, body, and spirit—I was a superhero.

Superhero status

I received the long-hoped-for telephone call three months after my final treatment. Carl is dead, evicted, and eradicated. I visualized this outcome, but it wasn't until I received the call that I released the breath I didn't know I was holding.

Now, it's on to the next goal: to share my story to help others. While modern medication was a tool in my arsenal, I believe my transformed mindset got me through to the other side. The other side is where the glass is NOT half-empty or half-full; the glass is refillable every day and at every moment, and I will fill it while wearing my Wonder Woman socks and cape.

Pep Talk

Linda's shift to a "superhero mindset" began with Gratitude! Gratitude changes the root thinking of a person. It changes our outlook and our attitude. Gratitude is a practice of looking for the good in everything, so that when life hits us with a sucker punch we can more easily and automatically find and focus on the good.

There's a universal law known as the Law of Polarity—everything has an equal and opposite. For example, there can't be a hot without a cold, an in without an out, or an up without a down—left without a right or a good without a bad.

We all know that stress is the number one cause of disease. If we understand this, we know how important our thoughts are to our health and our chances of fighting any disease in our bodies.

To say "think positive" or "focus on the good" usually isn't enough because it's at a surface level. We lack a fundamental understanding that if there's bad in something, there must be an equal and opposite amount of good in it, and it helps to know that the law makes it so. It's not toxic positivity. It's by law!

So, when we don't see the good at first (and chances are pretty good that we won't), we can be grateful for the good in advance, knowing that one day, we'll be able to look back and see the good that came of it.

If you listen to any successful person, they usually express gratitude for the darkest time in their lives, knowing that this brought them to where they are in their current success.

"There's something bad in everything good and something good in everything bad."

— Michael Lewis.

At peace with my past, at last

By Lisa Toma

It is incredible how everything comes to you when you need it. That is how I began my Wake Up Call journey. The journey would change my life and complete my healing process.

I grew up in a home where domestic abuse was prominent. I am the oldest sibling of four, and we felt it was our responsibility to keep our mother safe from her abuser, our father. We grew up in constant fear, unpredictability, and uncertainty.

Rewind to 2002, the first day of May was when our lives utterly turned upside down. The unthinkable happened, the forever nightmare. Our father murdered our beautiful, extremely loving mother, and the feelings of fear, unpredictability, and uncertainties were now more dominant than I had ever experienced before.

The following years delivered heartache, mourning, grief, insecurities, struggles, challenges, anger, resentment, and sadness. It was a long, long journey. After many years of grieving, I finally accepted that my mother was gone forever, and it was time for me to regain my power. I spent many years surrendering my energy to the tragedy that held me back from living, building my life, and being truly happy.

I met my wonderful husband, and we have three of the most incredible children. My life has a new meaning. I have three lives I love more than mine, and I never knew I could ever love like this. They give me purpose and inspiration to want to become the absolute best version of myself for them, and for me. I wanted peace. That's all I wanted. I wanted peace in my heart, peace in my mind, and peace in my life. I wanted to be the absolute best woman I could be. Once I surrendered, one thing led to another.

Coincidence?

I believe nothing is a coincidence; everything happens for a reason. Then strangers, now friends, entered my life and introduced me to the Wake Up Call.

The first morning I joined, a guest speaker discussed a novel and film he and his wife created called *The Ravine*. It is a true story of how their best friend murdered his wife and child. The narrative showed the arduous journey the victims of this tragedy had endured and the message of tragedy, healing, and forgiveness. Coincidence? I highly doubt it.

I felt it in my heart; this is where I should be. My awareness grew, and my yearning for more knowledge got stronger. I wanted to learn more. I wanted to grow, and forgiveness was the final step in my healing journey.

Just the thought of the word forgiveness made me cringe. I defined forgiveness as letting the person off the hook. I felt that letting my father off the hook would be a betrayal of my mother, family, values, and morals. Forgiveness was the one thing in which I carried the most resistance. It made me feel angry to even think about it. I knew I had to start somewhere. I knew this final step was the most crucial to set me free in my heart.

There was one of many things Joe said on one of the calls that inspired me to want to start my journey of forgiveness. The quote was, "What you don't fix, your kids inherit." That shook my soul. The last thing I wanted was for my children to inherit my anger and resentment. My goal is for my children to love life. They need to find the good and beauty in every situation. I want them to deal with their feelings and emotions in the healthiest way they can, and I was in no place to teach them that. I needed to give that to myself first.

I had to go deep within myself, and it was painful. I was on an emotional roller coaster, but I understand those emotions. To release my pain, I needed to embrace it.

The more I held on to it, the more it would catch up to me. I knew that holding on to the anger and resentment would cause illness inside my body and mind. It was a matter of letting go or allowing it to consume me, and everyone around me.

I had to do the work.

By consistently getting on the Wake Up Call every morning, journaling, private coaching calls with its creator, Joe Trimboli, reading, and self-reflection, I understood the definition of forgiveness. It was not letting my father off the hook or justifying his actions. It wasn't me calling him and saying, "Hey, I forgive you." Forgiveness was for me.

Instead of coming from hatred, anger, and ego, I learned how to come from a place of understanding, awareness, and acceptance. I understand everyone has their story and traumas. I gained an awareness that our thoughts determine our life. Everything we think about causes a feeling in our body, causing our actions and behaviour, continuing the cycle. If we continue to think negatively, we become prisoners of our minds without realizing it.

And finally, I learned how to accept that this is my journey and that everything is as it is. I can't change it or go back or control it. So, instead of remaining a prisoner, I set myself free.

I permitted myself to be vulnerable and to surrender to everything as it is. I set my father free from my mind, heart, and soul. I visualized him walking away and, in my heart, wishing him well, happiness, healing, and recovery from the traumas that brought him to do what he did to my mother. I felt more peace wishing him healing, hoping that no one else would be a victim of his crimes.

Instead of remaining a victim of my story, I embraced my story. I owned my story, and I used it as my strength. I became an advocate for survivors of domestic violence, and I became the voice of my mother and the many women who lost their lives and no longer have a voice.

I became a volunteer for a shelter for abused women and children called Yellow Brick House in Ontario, Canada, that provides life-saving services and prevention programs to meet the diverse needs of individuals, families, and communities impacted by violence. I coach children and youth through their struggles and challenges, and teach them mindfulness, resilience, confidence, and healthy emotions.

My goal is to share my story with the world and reach as many people as possible. I wanted to share my message to prevent more stories like mine and offer people the idea of hope and resiliency. I didn't know how I would do this or what it would look like, but Joe repeatedly reminded me that the "how" was none of my business, and everything would happen in ways I could never imagine.

I set my goal of wanting to reach as many people as I could and surrendered to not needing to know how it would happen. So I continued working on my growth, serving others, volunteering my time at Yellow Brick House and raising money for the shelter. And sure enough, just like Joe said, it happened in a way I could have never imagined.

I received a phone call from my contact at Yellow Brick House that a famous athlete doing some volunteer work heard my story and wanted to connect. She asked if she could listen to my story and find out how she could further serve the shelter and support their cause.

This incredible athlete was Bianca Andreescu! I met her via Zoom and shared my story with her. We spoke, cried, and developed a relationship over social media. She shared my story through her platforms, and we reached hundreds of thousands of people who felt inspired by my story. It was incredible. Letting go of the expectations of how I thought something should be, allowed everything to happen exactly how it was supposed to.

Since then, I have continued creating content on the struggles and triumphs of my trauma and have now reached millions of people. More opportunities keep presenting themselves, one of them being co-authoring Your Wake Up Call. I couldn't have planned it or imagined it to have happened this perfectly.

My message is to honour where you are on your journey, but don't stay stuck there. Heal your heart, set your intentions, serve others, do your work, and let everything else go. It will happen the way it's meant to be if you have faith. You have the power to co-create everything you desire if you focus on the good, remain grateful, and permit yourself to watch how magically everything will unfold.

Pep Talk

"Forgiveness does not exonerate the perpetrator.
Forgiveness liberates the victim. It's a gift you give yourself."

—T.D. Jakes.

Sounds nice, but HOW? How can anyone forgive such a horrible act? This is another area that requires our growth. We must grow into the person who is capable of forgiving. Lisa's story is one that sent shockwaves through our community and drove a stake right through our hearts. I knew how important forgiveness would be in her healing process, but also knew how uninvited the idea would be if presented prematurely. I would gently toss the idea out there, safely disguising it, directing it toward other people and scenarios, leaving it in plain sight, hoping she would pick it up and use it.

Sometimes a big enough "why" is the missing piece to what will make us willing to pay the price, or get us to do the thing we never thought was possible. Lisa's love for her kids and the magnitude of the idea, "what you don't fix, your kids inherit" created the awareness she needed to invite the idea into her heart. It also helps to know that forgiveness doesn't mean you have to have a relationship with the person.

The first step to forgiving is to open your heart and mind to the idea. If you think what the person did to you is unforgivable, remember Lisa's story and know it's possible for you too. As you work on yourself and continue to grow, you will acquire the strength and awareness needed to forgive and let go of resentment. It may be scary to go back and deal with past trauma but know that, *"The cave you fear to enter holds the treasure you seek"* — Joseph Campbell.

Remember that both resentment and anger are on a frequency, and you can only get what you're in vibrational harmony with. Remember also that the laws of the Universe don't know right and wrong. There is no right and wrong because everything just "is," so although you may be justified in your anger and resentment, the universe doesn't exempt you from the effects of the Law of Vibration and Attraction.

When Lisa forgave, she moved onto a better frequency and everything she needed to fulfil her purpose of reaching as many people as possible was on that frequency. She didn't have to go and find Bianca, Bianca came to her! We attract what we need when we need it. When she let go of "how" she was going to do it, she moved into harmony with the Law of Non-Resistance. Resistance indicates dissonance. When you focus on the cause, the effect will take care of itself. When you know this, you don't have to worry about "how" it will happen.

"Anger is like drinking poison and
expecting the other person to die."

— Buddha.

Why not me?

By Elvira Staltari

hy not me?

A question I could not allow myself to stop and think about. I was so caught up in my feelings of worry and fear that I didn't acknowledge that God was speaking to me. I see that now.

Many people would tell me stories of couples that had successful kidney transplants, intending to comfort me but would agitate me instead. I didn't want to hear it. It was all so overwhelming. For example, one morning my neighbour shared that he donated his kidney to a good friend more than a decade ago, and all I could think of was how? How do people do that? I think I've always felt it would be me donating a kidney. Well, I guess I worried it would be me. Surprise! I realize now why I paid attention to the stories of people on dialysis and how that affected their families.

In hindsight, those stories came to be the most helpful. My husband, Frank, never gave them any thought. He always did what the doctor told him. He didn't worry. That's what he would say to me.

As Frank's kidney function declined, I kept questioning why. I kept looking for answers I couldn't get. I guess I was looking for someone or something to blame because I could not control any of it. I was limited with what I was told I could do about it and felt defeated. At times, I felt guilty that maybe there was something I wasn't doing enough of. I felt I was missing something.

In September 2019, my journey began when my brother, Joe Trimboli, founder of the Wake Up Call, held a Mindset Workshop. That workshop led me to join his daily Wake Up Call. The call helped me look at things differently. I slowly realized the fears running wild in my mind. Although I've been given the grace of faith, I fight it. I worry.

I had a few breakthroughs, most notably the first call when we read *The Power of Intention* by the late Dr. Wayne Dyer. It was like a sucker punch, reading, "One who truly trusts God has no right to be anxious about anything." Well, Elvira, how dare you! If you have faith, then let it go; trust God, let God. That sentence quickly became a daily affirmation and my screensaver. I repeat, "I am not anxious about anything because I trust in God."

The Wake Up Call

The timing of these calls saved me!

So much was happening in our lives that the timing was divine intervention. I needed this material, and I needed to hear it. The material slowly strengthened what was inside me, learning to listen to my inner self, God within, and feel the words I was affirming.

The second breakthrough was during our reading of the book *Psycho-cybernetics* by Maxwell Maltz. It was when Frank's kidney transplant process had begun, testing family members to see who might be a candidate. His kidney function had declined, and we had considered the possibility of dialysis.

But no one was a candidate.

One Sunday morning, knowing what I did NOT want for my family, knowing with every cell in my body that dialysis was not a scenario I wanted for my family. I knew I would donate my kidney. I had surrendered. I had decided, finally.

One morning we were reading *Psycho-cybernetics* when the words on the pages came to life, I cried. "...You can figure out the best odds possible, or decide not to take the risk at all. But after the bets are placed, and the wheel starts turning—you might as well relax and enjoy it—thinking about it is not going to do one bit of good and is wasted energy."

I felt everything was going to be okay.

I had decided that I should stop thinking about it, don't waste any more energy, and imagine a successful outcome. At that moment, everything felt already done.

Frank and I would have a successful transplant and donation, and I needed to relax, stay calm, and trust. We had so many words of love and encouragement from friends and family, and I finally found the courage to speak with my children. I was always so worried about them. How would they feel? How would they handle the situation or react? How hard would it be for them to see their parents undergo surgery simultaneously? We were in excellent hands with the transplant team at the Toronto General Hospital. My children were in a good place. It was all happening.

I AM

I'd like to share one more breakthrough. Call member Silvio Azzinnari expressed how we need to be aware of our words in an essay he wrote. Specifically, the words that follow, I am. His I AM essay helped me realize I needed to be intentional in my words and thoughts. I knew the words I spoke could strengthen me. I am worthy. I am loved. I am valued. I am healthy. I control my feelings. I am focused on improving myself. As I get better, everything around me gets better. I can let go of any resentment and anger. Everything is happening for me. I am happy. I am calm.

Thank you, Silvio.

On the day of surgery, I can't describe the feeling of calm that filled me. I went in grateful, fueled by all the well wishes and our army of prayers I knew were behind us. As I write this, I am grateful that Frank is doing great, and I am as well. I feel the healing energy, the love and the blessings of a long, healthy life together. I don't have the words to describe it all.

This experience has taken a life of its own in our family. My children are comedians, and I'm thankful for that. I didn't decide to donate my kidney to hold this over Frank's head; he owes me nothing. I based my decision on what's best for my family and the quality of our family life. Many people have said I'm a hero, but the truth is, I'm not—I just did what I felt I had to do. What would you have done? I am lucky that I could help my husband. I am only the vessel through which God worked his miracle so that Frank had a match. The doctors and nurses who cared for us, the family who didn't leave our side during our hospital stay, and the family and friends who helped us during recovery; it's all so much bigger than any of us. I have learned that life isn't a series of why me?

Why not me?

It's knowing there is something bigger and believing it's inside us. There are always so many layers, and being in control of our thoughts is the most powerful and most helpful tool in life. Living from a place of love and gratitude is most important.

We felt so much love from everyone around us. It overwhelmed Frank and me with gratitude.

Worry and fear aren't something I have completely gotten a handle on. Some days get the better of me, and those emotions take over, but it doesn't last as long. With these lessons and my faith, my I AM affirmations, and the Wake Up Call, I am reminded every day of the importance of what you focus on–you strengthen, what you give energy to–grows, and how significant the words "vibrate higher" are. When we become aware of these things and learn to control our thoughts, it is life-changing.

Pep Talk

Information is constantly coming into our conscious mind, where we have the power to choose our thoughts, but that's not to say that we actually exercise this power. And that's where the problem lies. We don't know enough about the laws of the Universe or the laws of our being. When you study this material, you develop an understanding of who you are and your ability to think. You also acquire knowledge that will help you choose the right thoughts.

In the book *Man's Search for Meaning* by Viktor Frankl, he does an incredible job at proving that no matter the circumstances, the one thing we truly have that is our own, is our ability to choose what we want to think no matter what is going on around us.

We use our imagination to create scenarios in our minds. Those scenarios we imagine influence the frequency we move into, and we can only ever get what is on that frequency. This is why we usually get what we're expecting. What you put out; you get back.

What you focus on, you strengthen

Worrying is like praying for something you do not want. When you understand this, according to the Law of Perpetual Transmutation of Energy, which states that energy is always moving into form, you understand the importance of using your imagination to create what you want instead of worrying about what you don't want.

Everything is energy—including thoughts, so we create the energy that is seeking expression in physical form by emotionalizing the ideas we create in our imagination. As you become more aware and gain understanding, you develop a faith based on understanding and can more easily let go of what you cannot control or can, as you may have heard it said before: "Let go and Let God."

"God's plans for you are better than any plans
you have for yourself. So don't be afraid of God's will,
even if it's different from yours."

— Greg Laurie.

Who are you living for?

By Loredana Muia

As I was sitting on the edge of my bed in my new condo on the 32nd floor, staring out at a clear blue sky, I contemplated every decision that led me to this moment. I was in an environment one would describe as calm and peaceful, yet somehow, I felt everything but that.

I knew there was more to life than the one I was living—the one meant for me.

And the gut feelings and doubts I had pushed aside for months caught up to me. It left me with one daunting question. "Will I truly be happy continuously living this way for the rest of my life?"

I was newly engaged, had moved into my new condo, worked a job I enjoyed, and yet I knew I wanted more. I was on the path many would be happy to be on, so why was I left feeling so unhappy, alone, and lost?

I thought, "What's wrong with me? I should be grateful for everything I have."

Yet, I couldn't shake the feeling that something was missing. I knew there was more to life than the one I was living.

Growing up in a home where domestic violence and chaos were "normal," I was determined to fulfill one promise to myself: live in a happy, peaceful, and loving home. I lost my mother to domestic violence at my father's hands when I was 14 years old, which is something I will carry as my greatest lesson. It shaped me to be the woman I am today.

Following that afternoon of reflection in my condo, I surrendered to everything in my life. I decided to let go and trust that the universe would lead me to what was meant for me.

A new perspective

Weeks later, I entered the office of my new mortgage broker, Cristina. Little did I know, this was the day my life would change forever. As I looked around Cristina's office, sitting in the perfect spot to feel the sun's warmth beaming through the window on a cold February morning, I knew I was where I was meant to be.

From the calmness that ran through my body and my attention drawn to the yellow butterfly-framed picture on the floor up against her wall, I knew there was something more significant about today. Our half-hour meeting lasted two hours, and a lifelong friendship was born.

Cristina eventually introduced me to the Wake Up Call and assured me this was right up my alley. The Call is a community of people from all walks of life who study self-development and mindset books that teach us how our thoughts create our lives. This call was what I needed. All signs pointed to yes. I joined the community and have never looked back.

After the first month of study, followed by groundbreaking one-on-one coaching calls with The Call's facilitator Joe Trimboli, I understood my feelings about my life. I could no longer allow myself to feel guilty for wanting more. I came to terms with the first step to begin living my life for myself. I needed to put my happiness and peace first.

A month later, at 33, I was single, living independently, and beginning a new chapter. Society tells women that in their 30s, they should be well on their way to marriage, having children, and settling down. Although I was the furthest from that lifestyle, I was at peace knowing I had made the right choice. My life was just getting started.

What you seek is seeking you

As a result of my daily study on the Wake Up Call, I learned the importance of gratitude and developed the habit of daily gratitude writing. This practice helped me find the good even on the more challenging days—there is good in everything. The tough moments show up in life to teach us valuable lessons and help us grow into the people we strive to be.

The good came faster than I could have ever imagined. I was no longer financially struggling and could provide for myself, which I thought I would never do. Then, during a coaching call with Joe, my marketing background came up in our conversation, which sparked the next wave of new beginnings. Shortly after that call, I began working with Joe as the Executive Assistant for the Wake Up Call.

My new role introduced me to new friendships, life lessons, and a new self-perception, something I have always struggled to accept. I had created a life of putting everyone first and myself last. The happiness and peace of others were more important, or at least I chose to believe. I lived my life as a people pleaser, and at the age of 33, it finally caught up to me. My lack of self-worth led me to sit in my condo, asking myself, "Will I truly be happy continuously living this way for the rest of my life?"

A new beginning

I look back on the woman I was before I started my journey. I learned how to reprogram my thoughts, mindset, and beliefs. I used to be the woman who was hesitant about making a move, imagining what my family and friends would think of me, including the guilt of walking away from a life commitment I made to someone who loved me. I now realize I had promised to love someone before I truly loved myself.

To change, I needed to shift how I thought of myself and what I deserved. This year has been nothing short of breakthroughs, breakdowns, and life-changing lessons. I love myself and embrace the struggles and changes through gratitude, affirmations, and daily study. I am becoming the person I need to achieve my goals and create the life I desire.

We are on this earth to live our purpose, share our vision, and create a difference. We deserve to be happy. If I can help one person realize they have the potential and power to live to their fullest, I will have accomplished my goal.

The framed yellow butterfly picture sitting up against the wall in Cristina's office was more than a picture. There is a reason it was so significant to me. A butterfly represents rebirth, transformation, change, hope and faith. Since my mother's passing in 2002, my siblings and I have always referred to my mother as a butterfly. She is now free from the pain and suffering. Free, as she always wanted to be. I believe her presence was in the office that day, reassuring me I was on the right path.

We all have the choice to live the life we want. We can all create it. Decide what you want and go for it.

Trust your intuition.

Listen to your heart.

Our time is limited.

Please don't waste it living someone else's life.

Pep Talk

Most people are just going through the motions. Our whole lives, the people we trust and who love and care about us drill us with: "When are you going to find a nice partner? When are you two going to get engaged? When will you get married? When are you going to buy a house? When are you going to have a kid? When are you going to get a bigger house? When are you going to have another kid?" and so on. It's as though we just get on for the ride, never questioning what we really want.

Maybe we come to believe that's just the way it is. You make a business decision to go through life with someone, and maybe we trust that if we get on this path that our loved ones tell us to get onto, we'll be happy. We start living the life others want for us, and we wonder what's wrong with us! Why aren't we happy?

We hear things like, "Maybe you're too picky. Maybe you should lower your standards." How about this advice instead: "Grow into the person who can attract the right person. Get into a relationship with yourself before you get into one with someone else. Don't ever lower your standards. Follow your heart. Love yourself first so you won't ever have to depend on someone else loving you."

Why wasn't anyone giving us this advice? Why wasn't anyone giving us the advice Anthony Hopkins' character gave to his daughter in that airplane scene in the movie Meet Joe Black? "Love is passion, obsession, someone you can't live without. I say fall head over heels. Find someone you can love like crazy and who will love you the same way back. How do you find him? Well, you forget your head, and you listen to your heart. Cause the truth is honey, there's no sense living your life without this. To make the journey and not fall deeply in love, well, you haven't lived a life at all. But you have to try, cause if you haven't tried, you haven't lived. Stay open… who knows? Lightning could strike."

How many people just get on that bus and never get off because they don't want to let anyone down? They don't want to hurt their partner or their family, so they stay on the bus. How do you end a two-year relationship? How do you call off an engagement? Well, if you think that's hard—imagine how hard it will be after 10 or 20 years of marriage and a couple of kids!

"The heart has its reasons,
of which reason knows nothing."

— Blaise Pascal

The journey to discovering me

By Isis Seville

I would preach self-love but couldn't stand the sight of my body.

I was the emotional rock for my family, but I felt like I was crumbling inside.

Replaying my day would keep me up at night. I convinced myself that others were judging me. I knew I was blessed, but I felt overwhelming guilt for feeling down. I couldn't shake off the sadness.

There is absolutely nothing, and I mean nothing in this world that I love more than my kids. One day the thought, "They would be better off without me," crossed my mind, not in the worst way, but in a, "They deserve a better mom" way.

When that thought crossed my mind, I realized I had hit rock bottom mentally and needed to take action to help myself.

My life has been a struggle for what felt like a game of dodge, the anxiety version. As the eldest daughter of a South American immigrant family, I witnessed my parents' struggles and challenges in building a new and better life in a new country. I felt pressure from a young age to work hard; I wanted to make my family proud. However, with that came feeling stressed and anxious. Children could not openly express those feelings. Those feelings we didn't acknowledge or take seriously. Those were different times, and we didn't understand mental health.

I did my best to cope; suppress, suppress, suppress, and that worked out reasonably well. Sure, my body was screaming at me; severe joint pain led to the early lupus diagnosis, gut issues, migraines, hair loss, etc. But overall, from the outside looking in, I appeared as functioning.

I did well in school, worked hard at my part-time jobs, and got into my first choice university program. Life seemed "normal" to all who knew me. It wasn't until my mother's cancer diagnosis the year I was planning my wedding that things worsened.

It was a kind of stress and feelings that I did not know how to suppress, nor could I, but I had to because how could I possibly throw this onto my family dealing with the strain of my mother's health? I was scared, anxious, and depressed. For the first time, I asked for help. I turned to my family doctor and my fiancé; at that point, medication was the lifeboat I needed. I could pick myself up and be a support for my family once again. I could take my mom to her appointments, function and not feel like I was drowning in a sea of anxiousness and sadness.

As the years went by, my mother healed, and I married my best friend, the only one who knew about my struggles with mental health. We moved in and renovated our first home. We honeymooned in Thailand, and we were working our dream jobs. Life was picture perfect.

The familiar darkness returns

Cue motherhood, postpartum hormones raging through my body, and the familiar darkness; suppress, suppress, suppress. I would tell myself, "You can do this, you must," and somehow I managed. But I would secretly lock myself up in my room at work or home and breathe through a panic attack, careful that my colleagues and daughter would not see me. Sure, I could go days without leaving the house. Sure, I made plans with no intentions to see them through; dodged friends, ignored calls—I. LET. MYSELF. GO. Mentally, I was struggling. Despite that, I coped.

But in 2020, the world as we knew it changed.

Like many, I felt the effects of isolation. I felt the fear of the unknown and could sense myself losing control, but I was caring for two tiny people at this time. I was a mother solo parenting through a pandemic as my husband worked overtime as a first responder.

New world rules and regulations prevented me from having the support of my mother or mother-in-law. I couldn't unwind with my sister or friends and felt alone for the first time. I knew my girls were watching me, absorbing my energy and feelings, and I knew I needed to find something to help my mindset or continue winding down this negative spiral that I desperately did not want to go down. They deserved the best of me, so I needed to change. I deserved the best of me.

My soul was craving positivity and hope, instead of negativity and fear. That is when divine intervention introduced me to a community and a mentor that would change my life forever.

I have always felt drawn to personal development. As a teenager, I found comfort in books like *Chicken Soup For The Teenage Soul*. I read and watched *The Secret*. Something about those stories of regular people overcoming hardships gave me hope. I became a believer in the power of our minds and thoughts. I always knew the solution to my struggles would come from inside.

Early in the pandemic, I made a change and embarked on what would become my development journey.

The Wake Up Call

I discovered the Wake Up Call after surrounding myself with like-minded individuals who worked on their mindset. While in this community, I have undergone the most growth and transformation. I learned how to apply the knowledge to my life. One morning I heard, "What you don't fix, your kids inherit," which rocked my core. The mindset I had struggled with all those years was the last thing I wanted my daughters to take from me.

So I declared I would take back control of my thoughts and feelings. I learned to develop the skill of looking for the good, even through hardships and adversities. I learned to acknowledge fear, worry, sadness and doubt, to feel them, not suppress them.

I learned, through experience, that growing my mindset would be a work in progress as long as I live. Maintaining a healthy and fit body requires you to fuel it with the proper nutrition and movement, and a healthy and positive mind requires you to fill it with the right content. You must feed it material that will help you continue to grow your mindset and remind it of its potential.

Looking back at that person from two years ago, I realize how astronomical my growth has been. It is exciting to think that this is only the beginning. I still have moments when feelings of anxiety and fear surface. I believe it is part of being human, but now I respond rather than react, and I can work through those feelings more healthily and positively.

I have learned so much about myself, who I am, my true beliefs, and my purpose. I have mindfully manifested many positives and taken action on opportunities that would have terrified me in the past.

I wake up every day grateful for my life and the lesson. I am becoming more comfortable about opening up about my past. Everything I had bottled up was being released.

Many women find themselves where I was, scared and desperately wanting to make a change but not knowing where to start, not even knowing that they can turn it around. I will continue to share my story and strive to reach my goals, to show women that their potential is limitless.

Pep Talk

When we are not aware, our thoughts happen to us. We are not the ones in control of our thinking. People say, "I think this" or "I think that," but they aren't "doing" the thinking at all. The thoughts are happening to them.

Fearful thinking isn't something you do because if it were, you'd stop thinking about the negative things. Instead, you say, "I'm doing the wrong, negative thinking, and I can't stop." It's like you're possessed. You're not thinking those thoughts; the thoughts are happening to you. You are at the mercy of the energy field that produces the thought.

Every one of us has two images: the one we have of ourselves and the one we project out to the world. The inside doesn't always match the outside, which sometimes leads to feeling like a fraud. As you become aware, you begin changing your image of yourself; therefore, the energy field from which those thoughts happen begins to change. When you change your energy, you change your life.

"The day you decide you are more interested in being aware of your thoughts than you are in the thoughts themselves – that is the day you will find your way out."

— Michael A. Singer.

City to country

By Jennifer McCabe

A t 18, I joined the army as an artillery soldier. My interest in reading and personal growth began three years later during my eight-month deployment in Afghanistan. There, I read over 15 books on various subjects. After finishing my six-year contract with the army, I started my real estate career. I continued to immerse myself in other learning materials, including books, podcasts, and YouTube motivational videos.

Joining the Wake Up Call propelled me to another level and came when I needed it. In July 2020, I visited my mom in the hospital in Newmarket, Ontario. She was suffering from alcoholism and fighting for her life after falling down the stairs. It was one year after I had lost my father to brain cancer.

While driving back to Toronto, I locked eyes with another driver in the opposite lane—my childhood friend, Kally! We hurriedly pulled over to catch up after all these years.

Everything on the outside seemed fine. I had a successful career and a beautiful condo, but my family life was falling apart. I was burning out, emotionally drained from the past year and full of anxiety, thinking about what could happen next. I was lacking the positivity and focus I usually had. As I explained my anxiety to Kally, she knew what I needed—not a drink or a night out, but a 5 a.m. Wake Up Call.

The Wake Up Call was the accountability and community I needed on some of my darkest days. As my maternal family was falling apart, I formed a new one. I had the 5 a.m. community to lean into and be accountable to, feeling a duty to show up every morning and play full out. I didn't realize how much I longed for that until it showed up.

Examining books like *Outwitting the Devil*, and *Think and grow rich*, redirected my focus. It was the daily accountability and refresher I needed to get back on track. I knew a lot of this information from my previous readings, but I wasn't living and breathing it every day. The founder of the Wake Up Call, Joe Trimboli, could break down the new information and help me internalize it.

I used to read books to finish them and proudly place them on the shelf as a trophy of accomplishment. Today, I understand the value and importance of reading books for study, rereading them multiple times to reach a further level of understanding. Repetition is key.

An unconscious competent

Before being on the Wake Up Call, I realized I was an "unconscious competent." I was hitting goals by fluke, chance, or pure willpower, not realizing these things happen by law because we are in vibrational harmony with them. Joe's visual demonstration of dialling into a radio frequency hit the nail on the head.

Everything is energy, including thoughts. Learning the art of choosing my thoughts and shifting my imagination to focus on what I wanted, the best outcome instead of the worst is when things changed. I had a greater understanding of my life's successes and failures.

My results came from holding a particular image in my mind and getting in vibrational harmony with it. Whether good or bad, the laws of attraction would do their thing. I could set goals larger than myself. Instead of falling victim to the anxiety and "what ifs" of the past, I can blast through now. There is a sense of calmness and peace of mind, trusting and having an operating manual of how this massive clump of cells we call a body, works.

I have faith based on understanding. I did not need to fight, become anxious, or exert more force to get what I wanted. I needed to relax and keep focusing and taking action.

What I wanted

What I wanted was a lot more than being a realtor.

My goal card reads, "I am a top producing realtor in the Greater Toronto Area. I do so many transactions with minimal time and effort, so I can focus on my farm, animals, and helping people. I run a successful business on my land, attracting international guests and attention."

I went from a penthouse downtown Toronto lifestyle to opening an animal sanctuary on 10 acres of land 30 minutes outside the city. I facilitate various workshops, events and overnight glamping accommodation, while closing more real estate deals than I ever did while living in Toronto in the first year of joining The Call.

In the first year of operations, Hipcamp awarded me the best glamping site to visit in Canada. I had international recognition, press, and the pleasure of providing people with a safe space to connect with nature and animals during a global pandemic. I jumped into an untapped market at precisely the right time, providing the service and experience people desperately needed, creating a six-figure additional passive income for myself.

I knew it would happen by law

I knew it would happen by law, the same way it did when I was awarded 100% club and Platinum agent status within my brokerage Remax Realtron.

But with all these wins, the season of lows would come.

My mom succumbed to her addiction and passed away on September 18th, 2021, on my 33rd birthday.

If it wasn't for The Call, building a fortress of awareness and strength around my heart, this could have been an event that set me back to where I was in 2020. The Call fortified my higher mental faculties. I felt blessed to spend more time with my mom over the last year after moving her into my home to care for her. I could never have done it if I had stayed in my condo in the city.

I found solace and comfort knowing this too shall pass, recognizing what season I was in and found it easier to keep taking action, focusing on what I wanted and who I needed to be at this time. The real strength in character is who you are in the bad times, not in the good ones.

I am still learning and forever a humble student, but I can attest to the success I have experienced in such a short period, by applying the tools we focus on during the Wake Up Call. I don't allow my outside circumstances to control how I feel inside, and my imagination is powerful enough to emotionalize what I want. I am excited about my future because I know I am in control and creating it.

God created us in His image, which means we are Creators. So get creating the life you want! It's your birthright.

Pep Talk

When Jenny wrote her goal card, she had no idea how she was going to do it. The cool thing about Jenny is that it happened so fast. She was in harmony with the idea of owning and operating a farm where she could help people and animals. Jenny played a big part in bringing people from around the world to the Wake Up Call so she was already in harmony with attracting international guests. It wasn't beyond her self-image. She knew she was capable. When you're in harmony with an idea, it won't take long for you to see it manifest in your life. It's when we can't see ourselves with it, that it takes a long time visualizing to eventually accepting the idea.

Jenny's goal was so extreme but it happened so fast, and although it took work, it wasn't "hard" work. As the saying goes: do what you love, and you'll never work a day in your life.

Don't be afraid to set big goals! Actually, you should only set big goals! The only problem for you is that you will get stuck on the "how." Set a goal that's big enough to inspire you. There are two requirements for your goal:

1) You have to really want it and

2) You have to be willing to pay the price

Set the goal, and as you build the desire for the goal by bringing clarity to the image, you will find the next steps you need to take will show up!

Thank you, Bomber (Jennifer McCabe). I knew that I wanted to, "share this information with people all over the world." I never even had to think about how I was going to do it. You inspired members from Mexico, Thailand, the U.K., the U.S., and beyond. You've inspired us through your massive action and now you're enriching the world with your world-class glamping and wellness retreats. The Taiga is a special place and I know you're going to continue to help so many people there.

"When riches begin to come they come so quickly,
in such great abundance, that one wonders where
they have been hiding during all those lean years."

— Napoleon Hill.

Healing through Om

By Patti Persaud

As I reflected over the past several years, I was at a point in my life where I knew things needed to change.

I had been through some trying times. After having my second daughter, they diagnosed me with Lupus, an incurable disease. Lupus is a progressive autoimmune disease that attacks your muscles, organs, and joints. My rheumatologist made it clear—Lupus would be with me for the rest of my days.

I felt afraid and confused about my future life. I had a three-year-old and a newborn and was overwhelmed.

I had to figure out a way to get myself healthy.

Fast forward to 2018. After separating and reconciling with my husband I was in unfamiliar waters, but felt connected and surer of myself than I had felt in a long time. I had grown significantly from where I was, but I knew there was more, that I was meant for more. I didn't know how to get there.

Healing through Om

So I launched my yoga and wellness business—Healing Through Om. It indeed was a calling from my heart to be of service to others. But there was an even deeper calling itching, burning to come out. I had been on this path of self-growth and development for years, but I felt I had plateaued. I often asked myself, how do I get to the next step? How do I break through the self-imposed barriers?

As the universe always does, it brings you what you need in the most divine timing. I met Gail a few years ago, and she was ready for change. She understood I had been struggling and prepared for change.

She would often speak to me about a morning Wake Up Call and gently suggest that I should come on the call. She would say gently, "You need to get on this f@@king call!"

"What do you guys talk about? What do you do at 5 a.m.?"

She told me about a group of like-minded people studying self-development books to vibrate higher. I knew it was what I needed. Months later, in February 2021, I finally joined.

I noticed on day one how tight-knit this community was. Although it was a Zoom call, you could feel the energy. I felt their love and support. Why did I take so long?

Buddha's answer is, "When the student is ready, the teacher appears."

Everyone was welcoming and there to listen and offer support and guidance, with no expectations. Their honest desire to see you succeed and flourish touched me.

How could I have felt so loved and supported in such a short time? Was it my imagination? Was it possible that I had found a group where I fit in and belong, where I resonate within my core?

I began by setting my alarm every morning, and over a few weeks, I rose before the alarm. I was eager to see all those faces in little boxes on my screen, all those smiles that jumped through my laptop and grabbed my heart.

We read books like *Outwitting the Devil* by Napoleon Hill and *The four agreements* by Don Miguel Ruiz. We did the same with *Psycho-Cybernetics* by Maxwell Maltz, and Dr. Wayne Dyer's *Wishes fulfilled*, drawing deeply on their lessons.

As sure as my heart was beating, there was always a group member who would raise their on-screen hand and somehow be able to use these lessons in their life. I thought, how is this possible? How can they make such deep connections with a book and its lessons?

It happened to me

I had told myself that I was healthy and lupus free for years, but I didn't believe it. Then I made it my truth. I educated myself on ways to reduce inflammation and heal myself. My husband suggested I try extended fasting.

I no longer wanted to be on any medications. I had been on some awful drugs, such as methotrexate, an alternative method of chemotherapy. Doctors prescribe methotrexate in low doses for people with certain autoimmune diseases. These medications carry horrible side effects. I no longer wanted any part of it.

So I eagerly practiced intermittent fasting, then progressed to extended fasting. I also incorporated cold therapy, following Wim Hofs' teachings. What I saw amazed me. For the last 17 years, I would have my blood drawn and tested every four weeks to test my ANA's, ESR, CRP, ALTs, etc. These are all inflammation markers, liver enzyme counts and lupus markers. These numbers had always been highly elevated.

I am elated to say that in February 2022, all the numbers were in the normal range. My Lupus is in remission. After 17 years, I found a way that did not involve medication. When I saw my doctor, she was in shock. She said, "You always said you would beat this without meds," and I had.

So what changed? What shifted? It was all my mindset. I had told myself that I was healthy, but it wasn't until the last few years that I believed it deep in my core. I sit in gratitude of course, with myself, but I am so grateful for the Wake Up Call. The power of this beautiful group is like none other—knowing there is a collective of beautiful souls there for each other to guide and inspire, warms my heart. All I can say is thank you, thank you, thank you!

My yoga and wellness business has taken off. Over the years I have watched Healing Through Om grow, but this last year has been amazing. I have hosted over 30 local retreats since its inception. As I write, I'm at a yoga retreat created for ten beautiful women from the Wake Up Call; I am sitting overlooking Otter Lake in Muskoka, Ontario, Canada.

I just returned from hosting my first international yoga and meditation retreat in Costa Rica, a beautiful experience. Many more retreats are being planned for 2022 and beyond. My yoga community has grown, and I am honoured to hold space and guide others. My life has changed for the better since joining the call. I am at peace and living from the inside out.

I am so excited to see what the universe has planned for me.

What an incredible journey this has been so far.

And so it is.

Pep Talk

Patti's story is an incredible example of how anything is possible when you begin living from the inside out. We have the ability to reject any idea in our conscious minds. It is so important to understand that whatever idea we accept in our subconscious mind is what eventually takes root and shows up in our physical results. Remember that the subconscious mind is like the earth, it will return whatever you plant in it. We can choose the thought seed in our conscious mind, and by repetition, plant the idea in our subconscious mind.

We face the challenge of believing what we want to believe, in spite of physical appearances or current conditions and circumstances—in Patti's case, the diagnosis. If the thought seed is produced by current results, you can only get the same result. If you create the thought seed with your imagination, and use your will to focus on that idea, you will eventually produce that new result.

"Everything is energy and that's all there is to it. Match the frequency of the reality you want, and you cannot help but get that reality. It can be no other way. This is not philosophy. This is physics."—Albert Einstein.

So many people exert all their willpower on trying to change the outside world when our work should really be done inside. Changing the frequency involves changing what you're emotionally involved with. Changing what you're emotionally involved with involves changing what you're thinking about.

Information enters our minds through our senses. It is there that we take this energy that just "is" and make it what it "is" by the way we think. How we think depends on our use of our higher mental faculties. Remember that your paradigm, your current programming is in control of your higher mental faculties until you become conscious and make the decision to think on higher frequencies. You can look at a situation from the viewpoint of your goal achieved. How would the person that has your goal perceive the situation? How would the person that has your goal reason with things?

How would you feel from the goal achieved? Get onto that frequency and have that reality! Stop living by the medical report, the bank statement, the failing relationship, and create and hold the image of what you want in your mind. Create a crystal clear vision that you can get emotionally involved with. The feeling is the vibration, or in other words, the "frequency!"

"The power that made the body heals the body."

— B.J. Palmer.

A life of abundance

By Lucia Dekranian

Since a very young age, I have always been a free spirit, an artist, and a dreamer. Growing up in a small Armenian community in Iraq, I expressed myself through dance, singing, scouts and sports. As a somewhat introverted child, I still managed to do what pleased me at the time and live my life in such a way. This expression allowed me to create a sense of belonging within my surroundings despite the hardships of living through the war, and being restricted to the outside world from being unable to travel and experience other cultures and places. Living in this setting caused me to feel that I was not free, and I succumbed to a mindset of scarcity, a fear of not knowing what tomorrow held for me and just trying to survive day to day. I now realize and would like to share with you how this mindset affected me.

After we moved to Canada life became very different. My mother was a single parent who came from abroad with three children and we all moved to a small apartment. My mother worked two jobs to provide for us and struggled to keep up with the demands of our new lives in Canada, both financially and mentally. The money paradigm of scarcity was created; "Always save as much as you can" and "Hold onto it for you never know what can happen tomorrow." My mother was stuck in the paradigm that most of us are familiar with, constantly under the idea that money is scarce and preparing for the worst possible outcome.

I was raised with the mindset that we were not able to afford things or travel to places because of the fear of tomorrow, the fear of losing it all. Both of my parents and immediate family were formally educated in what would be considered in high regard through University and College education. Naturally, this was portrayed to me as being the only way to be successful. The old saying of, "If you want to make it, you should be a doctor or lawyer! That's the way to do it so you can make good money and live a comfortable life!"

My relationship with money

I have always been a strong-willed, ambitious, money-driven individual. I aspire to become a better version of myself and challenge myself daily. One of my biggest passions is to learn and master new skills.

When I turned 15 I got my first job. I developed a different relationship with money. I felt that money was somehow energy to me, the more I spent the more I made. I did not realize the true worth of money, and I spent it as I made it!

After high school I asked myself what made me happy and what I loved doing the most. Not acquiring a College/University degree was frowned upon throughout my upbringing, but I had a strong desire and feeling that something else was calling to me, maybe divine energy or a powerful force leading me in another direction. I decided that I should take some time off and do some soul-searching for what I really wanted to do in life. My search led me to my calling, and my first major career step was into the professional Make-Up, Cosmetic and Beauty Industry.

Opportunities started to present themselves to me. I learned to set goals and became an entrepreneur. I took on some amazing mentors to help guide me through my career, which led me to what would become the fruition of my calling. With all my newly acquired skills, I expanded and I grew. I became a Hair Artist and Stylist in the fashion world. Being in this industry as an Artist, my dreams were manifesting more and more. Travelling the world for destination weddings and media events, international magazine shoots, and having my work featured became my life. Loving what I did and offering those services that I enjoyed so much made me realize that this was finally it, this was my calling.

In my early 30s, I realized that there was a structure lacking within my money paradigm—I had no retirement plans, I lived for the moment, I worked hard and I played hard. I realized that all my hard work left me with no tangible assets to show for and no plans to acquire such. After accomplishing some amazing things in my life, a new paradigm began to develop in me. I had feelings that I was not good enough. I felt like I was not good enough to earn more money or to have a loving partner. I had a bad self-image even though it didn't look or seem like it on the exterior. I always had an underlying feeling that I was a failure. Comparing myself to others, I kept attracting people who were on the same frequency as me, and I wasn't growing any faster. Was this what life had to offer me and was I actually feeling like an imposter?

Life on pause

When the COVID-19 pandemic interrupted my business, I went from working six to seven days a week and travelling two weeks out of the month for the past two years, to now being home sitting idle for two months. It was like my life was on pause. I wasn't used to this new lifestyle change. I started to realize that I wasn't taking care of my health; being on the road constantly had me dining in hotels, restaurants, and bars. I never cooked for myself. I had developed health issues, I was diagnosed with cervical cancer and suffered from gastritis—I wasn't doing well!

I decided during the time I was forced to be off that this was my chance to really focus on myself and heal my body. Take this terrible situation and turn it into an opportunity to focus on the future and make some long-term lifestyle changes. Through some dedicated and focused research, I became educated in holistic healing; how to eat nutritious foods that heal and eliminate disease in the body. I got into working out at home with minimal gym equipment and cooking healthy meals, and I regained my health and felt like I was taking back control. Within two months I lost 20 pounds and felt amazing!

Being on this journey of self-love and healing, I realized I was changing and growing as a spiritual being; listening to my body, signs from the universe, and really being in-tune to my surroundings. People were noticing this sudden change. I started making new friends and breaking away from old ones. I was transforming, re-inventing myself, wanting to do more, and didn't know where to start.

The Wake Up Call

On this journey of self-healing, changing my morning routine was the first step. I started going for morning runs and reading more books. One day I was scrolling through social media, and discovered something called The Wake Up Call on a friend's page. I decided to join this amazing community of like-minded people. Learning and reading the most excellent material was resonating with my growth; it was Divine timing. The Wake Up Call became the perfect start to my morning.

Self-development came into my life when I decided to open a business. I started reading books and listening to self-help author Bob Proctor's teachings. I wasn't ready to invest money into self-development because I didn't think I needed it. That all changed when I met Joe Trimboli, the Wake Up Call founder and a Bob Proctor consultant. I remember feeling that this was the right time and recognized the signs that this program was being presented to me repeatedly. I joined Bob Proctor's Thinking Into Results program as well. The timing was right. I was ready. I took a risk.

One thing that stood out to me about studying this material is that we are all beings of energy; our body is a vessel that holds our spirit— spirit is pure, spirit is perfect. Our thoughts create our reality, and our body is an instrument of the mind. On The Call, we study the laws of the universe. As I started getting into this material, connecting my knowledge of quantum physics through my study of consciousness, yoga and meditation, I started to think about expanding my horizons and learning more about consciousness, which became my gateway to Ayurveda.

Ayurveda (the knowledge of life) was introduced to me through my research on healing my body when I was going through my health issues. I noticed that some of my clients had hormonal issues where they were experiencing symptoms such as hair loss and skin conditions. It all started to make sense. I started delving deeper into the world of healing the gut, and why all "dis-ease" comes from the body and mind not being at "ease."What could make all this throw off our balance? I dug deeper into the study of consciousness and how yoga and meditation, with the help of proper nutrition, can open our mind and connect to our heart to manifest our deepest desires, and heal us on a cellular level. Studying this material helped me expand my purpose—helping people heal from the inside and making them feel good about their physical appearance.

I did as the well-known motivational speaker Bob Proctor suggests, I had a goal, a deep driving desire. Our thoughts set up a vibration that manifests reality. A daily routine of affirmations, meditation, and working towards my goals helped me achieve my desires. The key is repetition. We have the power to create what we want in our lives. I believe I am a creator; I create my reality. My relationship with myself and my thoughts has improved.

I have a wonderful loving partner and a better relationship with my family; my career is taking off, and I have so much more to offer besides making people look beautiful. I know my purpose. There is a clear vision of my direction. I want to help teach people to heal through my knowledge as a health practitioner. I hope to have a beautiful and healthy world merge to create a space that can help people heal from the inside and look better on the outside.

I am grateful for the new opportunities.

My life is full of abundance.

Pep Talk

Remember what Einstein said? "Everything is energy and that's all there is to it. Match the frequency of the reality you want, and you cannot help but get that reality. It can be no other way. This is not philosophy. This is physics."

I suggest you read that again and again. I mean, Einstein said it!

Why wouldn't we want to spend some time understanding it? "This is not philosophy, this is physics." No one is exempt from the laws. No matter how smart or dumb you think you are, we are all subject to the laws of physics! You didn't go to school? You're not very tall? You don't know a lot of people? You grew up in poverty? Your environment at work or at home is negative? It doesn't matter! None of it matters! The only thing that matters is that you are a mass of energy and that by choosing your thoughts, you can move onto a different frequency and in so doing, can match the frequency of the reality you want and can't help but get that reality.

So many people are struggling, fighting with trying to change their physical results. In order to change the physical results in your life, you have to change the energy. In order to change the energy, you have to change your thoughts. It's your feelings that determine what frequency you're on. Think about the word "feeling". Feeling is a word we've given to describe our conscious awareness of the vibration that we're in.

I'll remind you here again:

Thoughts cause the feelings. Feeling is the vibration. Vibration determines the frequency that we move into! The stories you're reading in this book are all from members who became aware of things they didn't know before and were able to begin thinking differently as a result. They did this with everything they already had! This is why I'm so passionate about sharing this information. I know, without a shadow of a doubt, that every single person on earth is able to change their results and live a life they want to live. We've all been given unlimited potential! It's just a matter of becoming aware of who we already are so we can think into the results we want to achieve.

"As above, so below, as within, so without,
as the universe, so the soul."
— Hermes Trismegistus.

Your body is not a good home for a baby

By Sara Castelluzzo

"**Y**our body is not a good home for a baby."

I used to say this to myself repeatedly. I believed it in my core. So much so that I even voiced it to others out loud. How could I believe otherwise? All I have experienced in my so-called fertile stage of life proved that pregnancy and I were not aligned. I came to realize however, through the Wake Up Call, that proof is a questionable concept.

Is it proof of what we see, hear, smell, taste, and feel? During one of my pregnancies, my doctor told me my baby wouldn't survive in utero beyond 25 weeks. If my baby survived, I could expect severe health issues. I interpreted it as proof. After all, I heard the doctor's words. I saw the ultrasound.

I wish I knew then what I know now.

I wish I knew how powerful my thoughts were. When I took what the doctor said as truth and proof, my thoughts went in one direction and down a dark road. Perhaps if I understood that my thoughts and feelings had power, the conclusion of that pregnancy might have been different, or at the least my understanding and acceptance of what happened would have been different.

I delivered my son at 23 weeks.

He did not make it.

My miracle child

My miracle child was born at 38 weeks, healthy, strong, tiny, and a spitting image of his older brother, who is now resting peacefully. I realized that my healthy pregnancy was no accident. Two weeks before I knew I was pregnant, a job I had been working on getting for eight years came through. I was vibrating high. So I manifested a healthy pregnancy.

Finally, after five pregnancies I had a baby. I say five, but that part of my life is a complete blur. It could have been four or six. There is no timeline in my memory of the events, just many images, emotions, and words thrust together. I finally had this perfect miracle in my arms and brought him home. The first eight months were bliss. I was present with him. I was grateful for him and I was mesmerized.

Darkness follows me

But there was something in my head thinking that darkness followed me. Those wretched negative thoughts reared their ugly head. Things were not so blissful after eight months. I suspected my son had autism. And this is when I spiralled down into anxiety, questioning his every action and researching signs of autism. I blamed myself and said, "Your body is not a good home for a baby." Self-blame is a beast.

At age two, we officially diagnosed him. I accepted and embraced it. Today, he is thriving. I have realized that if I could have found gratitude in his uniqueness as a toddler and gratitude for my observations, which allowed me to find support for him, his care would have happened sooner.

When I contemplated trying one more time for another child early in my son's life, the data and science said the chances of having a second child with autism were much higher. I also thought I might miscarry again. The fear that I might have another stillbirth brought anxiety, doubt, fear, and the belief that I am not made for pregnancy.

I allowed those limiting ideas and thoughts to take over, and now at 42 I have my one miracle child of eight years old, and one heavy burden of guilt for not having the courage to try one more time to give him a sibling. I have been battling that guilt since his birth. Guilt is the current hill I am climbing today as I write this.

That voice that kept repeating those limiting words to me was an outside voice, not my inside voice, not my higher self. The voice was like the Devil trying to push me off track. Unfortunately, the Devil won. Now, I am beyond my child-rearing time, but I acknowledge the lesson—I will never permit a limiting belief to control me from this point forward. I will work to live from my higher self, not from external experiences or ideas. I have always felt I had a good connection with my intuition, but these past four months with the Wake Up Call have helped me communicate more confidently and clearly with that intuition.

In four short months, The Call has taken me from the bottom of the hill of limitation and guilt to the halfway point. The community and our readings and analysis have given me the strength and belief that I am ready, after 11 years, to deal with what I now come to realize is trauma. I've discovered various self-healing modalities and beautiful mentors on my journey to conquer that hill and return to the joyous and peaceful me I lost.

I wish I knew then what I know now

My subconscious told me that being a mom of two wasn't possible, that I am limited, defective, and essentially not created in God's image. But we are created in God's image. There are no exceptions. We have the power to heal, perform miracles, and co-create. God or Universe has given us so many beautiful gifts, including and not limited to intuition, will, and imagination, to create our dreams.

The ability to have children is the epitome of these gifts. I understand this now, but my negative self-talk hid these beautiful gifts. Instead of using these gifts, I used what I buried deep in my subconscious mind; the devoted belief and fear that my body wasn't a good place for a baby. This idea directed my major choices for a decade, or should I say, misdirected. I felt victimized, and bad luck followed me; that poor health was my fate. I was swimming underwater, holding my breath, desperately needing air. Now, with support, I am resurfacing and waking up.

I take time to focus daily. I meditate, participate in the Wake Up Call, journal my gratitudes, recite positive affirmations, and do physical exercise in the morning. As a result, my happiness set point has skyrocketed. I no longer suffer from debilitating anxiety. Not only did my anxiety dissipate, but I can also say I have found happiness. My family is noticing; I am a much better mom. I have my toolbox for life with all that I have learned and will continue to learn. I am well on my way to healing from my guilt and trauma. I have no intention of suffering from anxiety again and have much more awareness and understanding of living a good life.

They say lessons and teachers come when you are ready for them. I signed up for the Wake Up Call on November 25, 2021 (my 42nd birthday). Still, I didn't take part until January 2, 2022. I dealt with COVID-19-related anxiety that stopped me from doing even the simplest daily tasks. Instead, I participated in The Call when I was open to listening and learning. I hope my story is a lesson or a teacher for you. But if you are not ready for the task, re-visit my story when you are ready. It isn't going anywhere.

And I will be here waiting for you.

Pep Talk

We literally become what we think about! The problem is we've been programmed to live by our senses, what we hear, see, smell, taste and touch. These sensors give us information from the outside world about what's already done. If we let our current conditions and circumstances cause our thinking, we end up with feelings caused by those thoughts.

Feeling is the vibration we're in (good vibe / bad vibe). Vibration is a frequency, and you can only ever get what's on a specific frequency. Just like a radio station, you can only get whatever it is they are broadcasting on that frequency. You can't tune into the classical station and expect to hear rock music.

If you're tuned in to what is happening now, as in your current results, then you can't help but get more of the same type of results.

To say it differently; your results are causing you to think. Your thoughts cause your feelings. Your feelings cause your actions. Your actions cause your results—the same results you started with! And so, you can see how this becomes a vicious cycle.

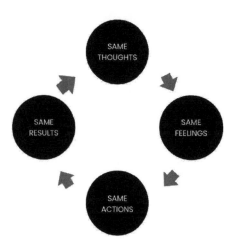

To create a new result, start with a new thought; a goal, an idea, a desire, the thing that you want! Let that thing be the cause of your thinking. Those thoughts will move you into a different vibration. That new vibration will cause different actions. That new action will get you a new result! You then observe the new result, and the new cycle is formed. The new result changes your beliefs about what you think is possible and your paradigm begins to change.

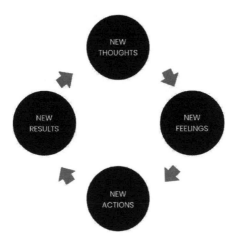

When Sara internalised what the doctors had told her, she tuned into that frequency and couldn't help but to experience the same result over and over again. When she landed the job she wanted, she moved onto a different frequency and experienced a new reality, even in other areas of her life.

What I love about Sara's story is how different her life is while the conditions of her outside world are still the same! She now can be more present and enjoy her little miracle who is absolutely perfect! She's changing the energy by changing her thoughts and is using her ability to create her world from the inside out!

> *"Change the way you look at a thing,*
> *and the thing you're looking at changes."*
>
> — Dr. Wayne Dyer.

My Wake Up Call revelation —it's life-changing

By Gabriella Amodei

When it felt like the world had stopped, my introduction to the Wake Up Call arrived. A global pandemic was amidst us, and the earth captured our existence, spinning it into the turbulence of online meetings on every subject available, in search of something.

I first heard about the Wake Up Call from a friend who interviewed its founder, Joe Trimboli. I had caught the last 20 minutes of the Zoom interview and felt immediately drawn to Joe's energy through the little square on the computer screen. A week later one February morning, I joined. I had no clue what this "Call" was about, but my curiosity got the better of me.

The group had completed reading *Think and Grow Rich by Napoleon Hill* and began watching a movie by the same title that first morning. The following morning, I clicked on the bottom bar to raise my hand. I didn't recognize my enthusiastic voice, but I was excited to be there.

I realized this group of like-minded people was what I was looking for. Little did I know how much I would learn about myself from being a part of this community. It excited me to learn that the next book on the list was one of my favourites, *The Four Agreements* by Don Miguel

Ruiz. It would be my fourth time reading it, and I looked forward to studying more.

"One little piece of misinformation can break down communication between people, causing every person it touches to become infected and contagious to others."

One sentence in the chapter, "Be impeccable with your word," hit home. After the reading, Joe gave his analogy. It wasn't until he said the line, "What offends you reveals you," that I realized I needed to look within.

I respectfully shut my camera off as I began to break down, so as not to look like a weeping fool. I recalled a past conversation where something someone had said offended me. The topic was not about me, but I let it fester. But why, on this morning, was I feeling its weight? It was something I needed to comprehend.

It's what Joe said one morning that helped me act. "Without a committed decision, you aren't changing the frequency." After the call, I felt an urgency to write a letter. I did not know to whom. Without prejudice, I needed to let it all out. I wrote until my hand felt numb. The tears overflowed. I felt a sense of release.

At this moment, I remembered another Joe-ism, "What you fight, you strengthen. What you give, you receive," and I realized I was fighting the wrong fight. It applied to all of my relationships. I could now see how this gave force to stories that were not true; mere fragments of things I kept fuelling to keep me in that lower vibrational state.

I got it!

Giving love to others meant giving love to myself. It was a concept foreign to me, and yet I know how impactful giving yourself love is, and above all else it is the most important step to forgiveness. It is one thing to know it, yet another to practice it. I commit to it every day.

Are my relationships better today than a year ago? Yes!

I have grown and learned to let things go that no longer serve me. Creating new boundaries for myself was a pivotal moment for me in my life. It has taught me how to mend relationships I didn't understand. There was something in this lesson meant for me. It gave me the clarity to let go of relationships that were no longer serving me. It was a substantial conscious awakening for me.

Realizing that I was okay releasing relationships with which I no longer had a connection was liberating. It allowed me to seek new friendships and make space for something and or someone new. It created expansion within the relationships that truly mattered the most, making them more valuable and profound and seeing them in a whole new light and attitude. They have all increased in value to me, and I am sure they have seen the change within me too.

It has allowed me to understand what being of service without expectations means. Now, when I am in a conversation I can take a moment to absorb what is being said, and decide how to shape my current vibration.

The Wake Up Call revealed to me the Laws of the Universe. They are an immense element in my daily life. I am aware when they occur and have fun with what source tells me, even when it is something that doesn't please me. I pay more attention to what I attract, think, and feel—putting my higher faculties to work. My life is not the same as it was before February 2021.

I added new habits to my life. I wake up with gratitude and journal every day, adding to my life's script as if it is already here, and I can tell you, it works in divine timing. I co-host a Sunday morning empowerment call for women, teaching yoga monthly and sharing my well-being thoughts and insights. Meditation has become a routine.

I changed my meal plan, began walking and released 12 pounds. I have also made strides writing my book. For the last three years I have been writing. I completed four programs in 2021: Certified Life Coach, Reiki Practitioner, Indian Head Massage, and Access Bars, which have increased my value from a regular hairdresser to an exceptional hair and soul healer.

What drew me to the Wake Up Call started as curiosity and now holds me accountable. I live with that awareness every day. I am a creature of spirit. Therefore, I have human experiences and know I can't always be perfect. However, I strive to be the best and live in love and light.

"You will face many defeats in life, but never let yourself be defeated." — Maya Angelou.

Pep Talk

"You cannot pour from an empty cup." You've probably heard this a million times—but what does this mean?

Many people don't love themselves and probably don't know it. Those that do maybe aren't really aware of how it plays out. If you're quick to say this is not true for you, consider how you speak to yourself or how you allow yourself to be treated. Would you speak to someone you love that way? Do you do things you really don't want to do, so that others will approve of you? If someone would've told me then that I didn't love myself, I too would've thought they were crazy. I know now that I really didn't.

How do you love anyone else if you don't love yourself? How do you give what you don't have? How do you have respect for anyone if you don't have any respect for yourself? If your cup is empty, you'll have nothing to pour out of it.

We have a filter through which we see the world. Suppose that filter is coloured by our insecurities, lack of self-worth, bitterness, resentment, etc. In that case, everything that happens, the way we see situations and others will be tinted by this filter.

If we don't love or respect ourselves, what kind of outlook do you think we would have of the world? How we think of others and how we treat people is a reflection of how we feel about ourselves. It's like jealousy—someone who is secure in themselves is not likely to become jealous as easily as someone who is insecure.

Everyone is either a friend or a teacher!

Gaby took responsibility for herself and as a result grew into the person that could learn from the important lessons we get from other people. It took Gaby a while to learn this lesson because we don't always learn the first time, and lessons will keep repeating themselves until we learn from them.

"There is a purpose for everyone you meet.
Some people will test you, some will use you,
some will bring out the best in you, but everyone
will teach you something about yourself."

— John Geiger.

97, 98, 99... ctrl + alt + delete... 1,2,3

By Fabricio Ramirez

I will start by telling my story. I was born and raised in Ecuador, South America, where I married and had three children. I had a happy childhood and youth. I always had a great relationship with my parents, siblings, aunts, and extended family. We lacked nothing and always had lots of love for each other. Unfortunately, my parents divorced when I was 15.

When I graduated from high school, I started my career in finance and accounting. I worked in banking for five years, in a car dealership, and for a couple of other companies as a controller until we came to Canada.

Project Canada 2017

In Ecuador, my wife was a sales manager for a rose export company, and her primary client was Canadian. Her company wanted to grow, offered her a job and sponsored her work permit. We made our decision within a half an hour and spent the following eight months preparing for our move to Canada. We sold everything and set out on a new adventure. We arrived in Oakville, Ontario, found a lovely house and had friends from Ecuador living close by that helped us adapt to our new country. When we settled, I started looking for a job and found one in 2018 as a controller. It helped me learn the corporate culture and further enjoy my Canadian experience.

We were in a good financial situation, but in 2020 my company reduced my salary but increased my responsibility, so I had to quit in February 2021. I thought it would be too difficult to get another job in accounting, so I reinvented myself. I started as a mortgage agent. Even though I made very little money, looking back I know it was the best decision I ever made.

Parallel to my story, things became complicated in my wife's job too. Although they sponsored her in Canada, they started mistreating, segregating, and undervaluing her. She was working over 12 hours a day. We knew she had to hold on to her job. We were on a work permit, and the company was processing our permanent residency. She couldn't quit, and her income supported my new career. It was a difficult situation, but she was always positive, professional, and strong in her endurance. She never made me feel bad about my new career.

As a mortgage broker, I started on fire with three deals from friends, but afterwards, it got tricky. It was hard to find clients and referral sources. I became impatient and felt a lot of stress for not contributing with the house expenses.

It was the visible part of the story, but what was happening inside me? I thought I knew it all and could figure everything out. I needed no help, and especially not self-help. My luck, my teachers, my former bosses, everyone was to blame. I was the person who would find an excuse for every good idea, and at the first problem, I would begin to surrender. Negative thoughts equal negative vibrations and end in negative results.

The Wake Up Call

When I discovered the Wake Up Call, I tried it. I woke up at 5 a.m., turned on my laptop, started the video conference and I listened to an audiobook called *Outwitting the Devil* by Napoleon Hill. That book had clear thoughts and ideas and I got hooked. I realized my problem was my mindset, and I had to reset it!

So I woke up early every day, but I didn't believe that things could change. An important moment was the first call I had with Joe Trimboli, the call's facilitator, when he told me he believed in me. I was going to sell a boat I owned to pay for Bob Proctor's *Thinking Into Results* (TIR) program. Boating is my passion, and I didn't really want to sell it, but Joe said, "I can see you really want it. Keep the boat, and I will finance your program."

I couldn't believe he was betting on me without really knowing me. There was something special about this program. TIR is a program designed to facilitate positive, profound, permanent changes in any area of your life. So, I signed on and started my process of becoming aware and understanding the universal laws, hoping it would happen like a miracle.

As part of my TIR coaching program, I had monthly calls with Joe, where I would complain about my situation and try to get tips for my mortgage business. Some months later, I called Joe and complained that I was sending gifts to referral sources and didn't even get a "thanks" from them, and he asked, "When was that?"

"Three weeks ago."

"Give it time to get a reaction. Let the Law of Gestation work."

The second I hung up the phone, a realtor called to give me a referral. In that month I got seven application referrals from different realtors.

The breakpoint

In January 2022, I sent Joe an email with some points I wanted to discuss during a call. When we started the call, he said in a firm tone, "We're not going to spend our time talking about the negatives today."

I didn't understand what he meant. We started discussing my mindset and strategies to get more clients. He sent me the recording of the meeting to watch. After watching it, I realized I was always focusing on problems, not solutions. I understood what Joe had said so many times: "Everything has both good and bad in it. Focus on the good."

Things improved in my mortgage business, with more calls from clients, consolidating relationships with my referral sources and being busy with a couple of deals in the pipeline.

In February 2022, at my wife's company, the owner and the vice president from the head office in Miami came to Toronto and restructured the company. They realized the value and knowledge she had about the business and industry. She felt empowered and began a new chapter. Her effort and patience paid off. When the owner was leaving, he asked her,

"What is Fabricio doing?"

"Mortgage broker," she replied.

"Wasn't he a controller back in Ecuador?"

"Yes."

"Tell him to call me tomorrow. He will not regret it."

That night when my wife told me, the first thing that came to my mind was that in 2018, five months after we immigrated, I told her, "You should tell the owner that you and I can look after the company for xxx amount, and we will take good care of the company." Then I said, "Bahh, that's impossible. A husband and wife in the same company!"

They didn't know me, so the chances were zero!

Now things are almost as I imagined. My wife has more responsibilities and an essential role in the company, and I am the director of finance.

My biggest change? In the past when I faced a problem I got paralyzed and tried to escape. I know that I don't know everything, but I will take on any difficult situation. Things will come to me at the right time, and I will succeed. Look for the good! I know the path.

Dedicated to my abuelito (grandfather). A kiss to him in heaven!

Pep Talk

It's amazing how many times I ask, "What do you want?" and after a few words, the person goes on to talk about everything they don't want. How it's been. How it happened. Why it can't be any other way. The question is simple, "What do you want?" Yet to focus on that seems nearly impossible.

Listening to people answer this question makes it easy to understand why so many people are stuck. Going back to what Ralph Waldo Emerson once said, "The only thing that can grow is the thing you give energy to." Most people keep giving energy to what is already going on in their lives. That means you can only get more of the same. Basically, you're stuck.

You can perform miracles in your life if you can create the image of what you want in your mind, and then focus on that despite the appearance of what your senses are telling you. In order to do that, you need to be aware of things you cannot see: Truths and laws of the universe, to support your thinking. In this case the Law of Gestation states there is a period of time that all seeds need to pass before they can be harvested.

We do something and become discouraged when it looks like nothing is happening. When Fabricio gave gifts to his referral sources, it only appeared like nothing was happening. When you emotionalize that illusion, you move to a negative vibration. It is like planting an acorn and digging it up after a couple of weeks because it looks like nothing is growing. Obviously, doing this destroys its growth.

Understanding the law allows you to stay focused on your image, trusting that everything is happening in perfect time; that the invisible is moving into form. When you begin thinking more about what you want and feel it, you begin to see more of that manifest in your life. Stop talking about what you don't want and begin thinking about only what you do want, and be patient!

"Patience is not the ability to wait, but the ability to keep a good attitude while waiting."

— Joyce Meyer.

A beginning of a beautiful journey

By F.F.

It was a hot summer night in the year 2020. I had just put my daughter to sleep and lay with her for a little longer. As I was with her, I stared at the ceiling thinking, "How will I provide for my daughter with only a few dollars to my name?" I was broke and depressed.

It all started three years ago when my ex, the father of my child, kicked my daughter and me out of his house at midnight. I was now living in a shelter with my two-year-old daughter. I thought I had hit rock bottom.

But it was the beginning of my path to healing myself.

That hot summer night of 2020, my anxiety was kicking in. With no money, I quit my full-time job, and the business I had started was not producing any results. How could it? I lived in a victim mentality, and my daughter was at home full-time because of Covid-19. "There is no way I can come out of this shit hole," I said while opening a bottle of wine. Wine always helped me escape from my sad reality. But guess what? The morning after, I had a massive headache, and my problems were still waiting for me.

I was drowning in my negative thoughts, excuses, self-pity, and always being the victim. I blamed my parents for not raising me well. My ex left me alone to care for my daughter, and I blamed him too. I even blamed my daughter for being born. So, as the days went by I kept turning to the wine bottle and waking up feeling even worse. The year 2020 went by like that. I only made two sales that year.

A dark place

It got so bad that I would run away and drown myself in drinking and drugs—anything to numb the pain in my heart whenever I had an opportunity. I realized how much my past was ruling my life. I knew I didn't enjoy those nights because I felt shame, guilt, and anger when the high wore off. How can I do this to myself and my daughter again? I would sleep in the car the next day because I was too ashamed to face my daughter and my mom, who was taking care of her.

Throughout that year, my inner voice grew stronger and stronger. 2020 took me to a dark place where I faced my demons. It forced me to look at myself in front of a mirror while telling myself the truth. My soul was hurting. Every day, I would stare into my eyes. I know it sounds creepy, but that is the only way you will never lie to yourself.

Change is coming

The nights were colder. Darkness set in at five every night. I was never a big fan of those nights. But this time, it felt like a change was coming. In January 2021, I decided not to drink for one month. It was the first time I didn't make any New Year's resolutions. It was what my soul and body wanted and needed.

So for the first time, I changed my perspective. I stopped blaming others and quit being a victim. I took matters into my own hands and found work.

I turned it around for myself and my daughter. It was my best year in terms of work. I exceeded my financial goal and won a platinum award.

But by the end of 2021, I was exhausted and burned out. I was making money. I had more stability, but something felt missing inside of me. It almost felt like my soul needed something else. I wanted to be a part of a community. I desired to wake up early, read more, meditate, and reflect.

I took matters into my own hands. I decided to put it out there.

By now, I had some idea about the law of attraction. "What you think about you attract." I put it out in the universe on my Instagram story.

"Looking for some advice/ideas on how to wake up early in the morning," and a few minutes later, a friend on Instagram recommended that I join Joe Trimboli's Wake Up Call. And I did!

My morning routine began.

I now have time to reflect and be grateful. This community gave me the beautiful gift of reading. I don't think I have ever read so many books in such a short period. The Wake Up Call community has taught me to be patient and accept how I am—the good, the bad, and the ugly!

I no longer open that wine bottle. I believe my wishes are coming true. It is the beginning of a beautiful journey to live a fulfilled life with my daughter.

Pep Talk

Everyone who's ever accomplished anything of relevance will always look back and express gratitude for the darkest, most difficult times in their lives. It is the beauty of contrast. How would you ever want heat if you didn't experience cold? We've heard it before, "You get motivated by desperation or inspiration."

In desperate times you may become motivated to make some changes—to take 100% responsibility for your life, to let go of the excuses and all the reasons to stay where you are. I never suggest anyone takes blame for what someone did to them. Don't ever feel like you attracted the bad. We can't control what others do with their free will. We can't control what happens to us, but we can control what we do with what happened to us. We can take control of who we're going to be in the face of adversity, and if we come to accept and truly understand the law of polarity, we know that Napoleon Hill was right on when he said,

"Every adversity, every failure, every heartache carries with it the seed of an equal or greater benefit."

Key word, "seed!" We have to plant the seed and nurture it. We have to find the good in the situation, and often, we can only see it when we're looking back.

> *"Sometimes when you're in a dark place you think you've been buried, but you've actually been planted."*
>
> — Christine Caine.

My wish

By Adriana Romeo

My name is Adriana. I have been married to my high school sweetheart for 22 years. We have two beautiful children, 19 and 16. We live on a farm with a toy poodle, a horse, and two goats. I have been working as a mortgage specialist for 18 years. I am grateful for my career, as it has given me the flexibility to be front and centre for my children, my family, and any extracurriculars.

In 2005, I nearly lost my life giving birth to my son. They diagnosed me with placenta previa, and at 33 weeks my placenta erupted, sending me to the emergency ward. On the way I remember hearing the paramedics say, "She is going to faint," and, "This is a time bomb!" My son was born at 5.5 pounds, but with complications. Thankfully, with the help of doctors and my mom, we made it through.

My mom was my best friend, advocate, confident, and my first and last call of the day. We could talk for hours about everything and nothing. My mom was a two-time cancer survivor—at 30, with cervical cancer, and at 46, with breast cancer.

My daughter and I took my mom to her chemo treatments during the 2002 to 2004 SARS outbreak, so we could not go into the hospital. We would drop her off and wait. Later, when she lost her hair, she asked me to take her to get a wig. I said, "Mom, are you sure you want me to come?"

"Of course!"

Tears rolled down my eyes as I watched her hair fall to the floor. She confided in me that my daughter gave her strength during the treatments. When my daughter turned one, my mom finished her treatments and shortly after was cancer-free.

We spent almost every day together, the three of us. It was simply the best time; we laughed and cried. I have so many cherished memories.

In 2012, my mom's cervical cancer returned.

Initially, doctors thought it was a urinary tract infection. Her symptoms would reappear after a couple of months. She insisted on seeing a specialist and had a biopsy done of her cervix. She had never heard back.

In January 2012, my parents went to Florida. They had recently purchased their retirement place and had been there two times before. My dad planned on retiring early to spend time with my mom and our family. When they returned, her symptoms reappeared, and after visiting her family doctor, she found out that her biopsy had revealed a reappearance of abnormal cells. She told her doctor (the same doctor who delivered me) that she was finished. We remained positive because we believed she deserved a miracle.

Why a miracle?

My mom belonged to The Catholic Women's League. There, she donated her time and love to the church. She taught the rosary in elementary schools almost every day. She would give her last penny, the shirt off her back, and a meal to anyone who needed one.

Every year, she would bring food and gifts to families in need. She devoted her life to her husband, children, and grandchildren. She was a saint on earth; anyone who met her would immediately feel peace. She was always there for everyone with all her heart, being that shoulder, no matter what. She never complained about her illnesses (she also had IBS), her pain, or her suffering.

About three weeks before she passed, as much as I thought she would survive during her suffering, I said, "This is not fair! You don't deserve to suffer."

"Adri," she said, "Jesus died on the cross. This is not suffering."

I was with her every day, and I promised her I would do everything I could to save her. Every day I prayed. My heart would hurt because I prayed so much. I reached out to so many medical professionals who treated her. I believed my wish would come true because my mom deserved a miracle to be cancer-free, to live to see my children and her other grandchildren grow up.

My failure paradigm

After losing my mom, my failure paradigm came up. I held a lot of anger towards myself and lost my faith, because I promised I would not let her leave. My wishes and prayers should have been answered. I went downhill, developing chronic back pain, and was soon diagnosed with rheumatoid arthritis in my lower back. I gained excess weight being on certain meds. My relationship with my family was falling apart.

One day, seven years after my mom's passing, I decided to change my life. I was a young mom who could not walk around a mall for more than 20 minutes without sitting or popping a pain relief tablet. So I hired a personal trainer, started losing some weight, and got off all the meds. I regained my self-esteem and confidence.

One of my retirement goals was to become a yoga teacher. When my daughter was one, I went to yoga. It helped me mentally, emotionally, and physically. One day I had an ah-ha moment; I realized my mom never made it to retirement, so why am I waiting and denying service to others? So, I signed up to become a yoga teacher and graduated in 2020 during the COVID-19 pandemic alongside the most amazing soul sisters I hold dear to my heart.

The guilt did not go away

I had failed my mom. Then one of my high school best friends, Cristina, asked me to join her for a daily wake-up call at 5 a.m.

"Girl, I am not waking up at 5 a.m. for a call."

But I noticed her growth, so I joined.

Wow! What a community.

It's about personal growth, changing your life, and transforming. Every person I met on the call became an inspiration. Now, every morning, The Call sets my day.

One morning The Call's founder and leader, Joe Trimboli, told a story about his sick friend and how he spent time with her. His friend was giving up on life, and he helped her. I was emotional, thinking of my mom. I was angry, to be honest, as I felt my mom deserved another chance, and I did everything I could to save her. Until I learned it was the law of cause and effect; what we put out, we get back. My mother put out ten years, and that's what she got—ten years. It was not my wish to be answered, it was hers.

When mom had breast cancer, I learned she had asked God for ten more years. She told me before being diagnosed a third time, "Adri, if I get sick again, I won't survive. My body won't be able to endure the treatments again."

She knew.

Mom had asked for ten more years of life—God fulfilled her wish. I felt as though 1000 pounds of weight had lifted off my shoulders. I could breathe again. Today, I live without guilt. I have the most beautiful spiritual relationship with my mom.

Thinking Into Results

When I hired Joe to coach me through Thinking into Results, a system created by self-help author Bob Proctor to bring changes in any area of your life, I began organizing my life, goals, and dreams. One of my goals was to marry my financial and wellness careers, and quickly I became in harmony with this goal.

Joe walked me through what my day should look like, asking for more help in my financial career (removing the things that I did not need to do), and opening space to teach yoga.

One day I will have my big goal, a financial wellness centre; it already has the name Heaven on Earth. Heaven on Earth will be a space for everyone, including cancer patients.

During my time with my mom at the hospital, there were patients I met who were alone, and I wanted to offer them a place where they could live and do yoga, get reiki treatments, have life coaching sessions, and get financial help.

With the help of my angel mom and other angels I have in heaven, and with the Wake Up Call community, Heaven on Earth will open its doors on my farm.

Until then, Namaste.

Pep Talk

It's not uncommon for people to feel guilty when they lose someone they love. Usually, this guilt comes from the person having said something they regret or not having said something they wish they had. For Adriana, it was the feeling that she could have done more for her mom or done something differently to prevent her from dying.

Guilt is a normal emotion of grief, and although it's not always rational, it's a real emotion. The thing about guilt is that it sits on a very low frequency, where all the other stuff on that frequency exists i.e., rheumatoid arthritis, chronic back pain, deteriorating relationships, weight gain, etc.

When we feel guilt, we unknowingly "choose" to build a negative idea in our conscious mind, and then allow ourselves to get emotionally involved with it. Without awareness, the guilt continues because we don't stop to discredit the reasoning. Thankfully, Adriana became aware of certain things that allowed her to take a different perspective, and rid herself of the guilt.

Results can and do change this quickly. It can happen as quickly as turning the dial on your radio to a different frequency. You receive a very different broadcast on a different frequency, and we can do the same with our lives.

"Guilt isn't always the most rational thing. Guilt is a weight that will crush you whether you deserve it or not."

— Maureen Johnson.

Burn out

By Stephanie Soave

et me start by sharing where my life was before I woke up.

I was a multitasking mom with two children aged three and five, a wife to a hardworking husband, and a full-time real estate broker managing the demands of my business. My children were happy and healthy, my real estate business had taken off, and I was a top-performing agent. My husband and family were proud of my accomplishments.

But people didn't know how much I sacrificed personally and with those I loved.

I worked around the clock without boundaries, fully committing to clients' needs and pouring from an empty cup. I was exhausted and going everywhere but nowhere. The days would pass, and I'd forget what day it was. I thought it was a compliment to be busy.

I could barely keep up. I come from a family who pride themselves in working hard; being overworked and burning out was a sense of accomplishment. It meant that you were doing something right. "Don't complain. Don't be ungrateful. You never know when the rainy days will come."

I also knew what it meant to struggle and come from a lack of money. My husband and I had times when we were unemployed. We would have to find a way to pay our mortgage when we first had our children.

We never wanted to return to those days again, so overworking and self-sacrifice were necessary. Rise and grind was a typical saying.

How could I say anything was wrong? "That would be selfish of me," I would say. We were doing well, and from the outside, everything looked good. The truth was, I wasn't living a healthy lifestyle, and my career consumed my life. My kids and husband felt it too. I spent weekends and evenings locked up in my office, working until midnight. I missed many extracurricular activities with my kids, their most significant milestones, and their memories. I would often come home to my kids and husband waiting on me for hours, only to disappoint them time and time again.

Most mornings, I woke up after the alarm clock. It meant rushing to get the kids to school, yelling and being angry as if it was their fault. My behaviour often left me feeling guilty because I was treating my children and husband poorly.

I knew this wasn't the life I wanted to live. I couldn't. It was utterly unsustainable. There were only so many empty promises I could make to my family. Although I didn't know it then, I was on the verge of a nervous breakdown. I found every excuse for being busy and what I thought was productive. I began making excuses for my actions and why everyone else was wrong but me.

I couldn't continue like this! As a mom, I felt guilty for not having time with my kids. As a wife, I was not present in my relationship and wasn't feeling good about my health. I needed something to change, but how?

The Wake Up Call

I remember the day I spoke to my friend Lisa, a mom in my neighbourhood. One morning she introduced me to the Wake Up Call and said, "Steph, you've just got to try it." At first I couldn't even fathom waking up at 5 a.m.! I remember thinking to myself, "How am I going to do this? Why would someone wake up so early?"

Finally, after a week, I gave it a shot. I had nothing to lose after all, but potentially something to gain. After the first morning, I couldn't believe the information shared. I looked at the Zoom screen and counted over 100 people. I remember walking away from my first morning thinking, "Wow, I have been asleep for so long."

How could I have been asleep for so many years? It was the beginning of my self-development journey. A few days into this new routine, I heard the Call's founder, Joe Trimboli say, "What you don't fix, your children inherit."

Boom! That was it. It was a big life-altering moment that caused me to shift and change how I approached my personal and professional life. It was not the life I wanted my children to inherit, and I needed a shift. I was ready to put in the work. It needed to happen.

This wake-up moment allowed me to reflect on my life. The way I was running my business, the way I was showing up as a mom and wife and for myself needed to change.

I started waking up at 5 a.m., studying principles, being on the Call, journalling, and exercising before starting my day—waking up before my kids gave me time to be more prepared and ready to take on the day. It allowed me time to visualize, write my gratitude, and think about what I wanted.

After applying the principles learned through reading and studying, my life improved drastically in only a few months. I feel like I am stepping into my fullest potential. My business has grown exponentially. I am hiring out and leveraging. I own my real estate team, which has given me back my weekends with the family.

We are vacationing more and seeing friends and family. My relationship with my husband has improved. I have made new friends. I have been on yoga retreats for personal care. I feel so much gratitude and energy. My mind, body, and soul I've nourished. I can picture what my life by design will be like in the coming years.

And it is breathtaking!

Pep Talk

There it is again, that heart stopping statement that we've heard a number of our co-authors make reference to, "What you don't fix, your kids inherit!" How many ways are we thoughtlessly forming who our kids are becoming? What are we saying, how are we behaving, what are we doing while we're on autopilot—when we're not thinking? While we are being blown about by everyday demands that we are constantly reacting to?

We are constantly reacting to everyone's needs: client texts, emails, phone calls, appointments, meetings, and fires to be put out. Then we have our families that depend on us, and kids who need to get to practice and school. We have parents we want to see, especially since we know we'll feel guilty later if we don't. We're never creating when we're constantly reacting to the outside world, and eventually, we have nothing left to give.

Taking care of ourselves first can feel selfish, but that's because we lack the understanding. We hear it each time we get on a plane. "In case of an emergency, put on your own mask first before assisting other passengers." It makes perfect sense when you think about it! You can't help anyone for very long if you don't make sure you get what you need first! This is a new way of thinking. It takes breaking out of the habitual way of doing things and intentionally matching our actions with what we want!

> *"Sometimes being selfish is the most selfless thing you can do, because it's only when you take care of yourself can you truly take care of others."*
>
> — Unknown.

Living life at my own pace

By Kristina Bothmer

What would life be like if I wasn't here? As I lay in my dark room, that question would run through my mind every morning. I had never said this out loud or acknowledged that this was a question I needed to understand if I wanted a life of truth and love.

In 2019, I went to a regularly scheduled check-up with my family doctor. I love her. She is everything you want in a doctor. During routine blood pressure checks and small talk, I started crying. You know that kind of ugly cry when you can't stop? It was at this moment I recognized I wasn't okay.

I was a single, 32-year-old elementary teacher living alone in a rental unit and had no children. It is how I used to define myself. Isn't that sad? I would dwell on these factors, thinking that I am unlovable, too old to have children, renting isn't as good as owning a home, I'll never meet anyone.

I constantly compared myself to those around me who owned homes, married, had babies, and moved on with life as happily as possible. How can an educated woman like me, with an amazing career, loving parents, and friends who care deeply for her, think this way about herself? It's because society embeds these things in our subconscious. If we don't have a child by 35, we better get on it if we ever want it to happen, social constructs seem to say. We simply accept that this is the way to live and if we don't fall along this path, we aren't worthy or good enough. My subconscious mind accepted this programming. I saw it as the norm.

Many likely never have these thoughts because they did follow the yellow brick road society has planned out. They have a family and place they call home. On the flip side, others who are single have learned to love themselves and accept that their yellow brick road is the road meant to be. I didn't fall onto either of these roads.

People in my life would describe me as incredibly positive, confident, and a light that shines bright. My friends and family had no idea how sad and depressed I was. My therapist of seven years was the only person who knew. I would call her for an "emergency session" because I couldn't deal with life. I'd start crying and couldn't stop. I hated the life I was living. I'd often drive to my therapist to discuss one of my many toxic relationships. I didn't always have the best partners. I didn't feel respected the way I believe someone should feel in a loving partnership. I now understand that I stayed in these relationships longer than I should have. Ultimately, I wanted someone to love and care for me. I didn't love myself, so I needed someone else to love me. I was lost, resentful, and unhappy.

The Pandemic

Then, the pandemic hit. Being a teacher and seeing my students was the part of my life that genuinely filled my heart. However, school routines, fulfillment, and normalcy weren't there for me. I had to work from home and teach through a computer screen. I would then spend my evenings and weekends at home, alone. The events with friends, workouts at the gym, dinners out, and get-togethers that also used to bring me happiness were no longer available. My anxiety was at an all-time high. Depression had taken over.

I had two choices. The first was to continue being miserable, and the second was to do something about it. I chose the latter.

I turned to social media; I was already bored of Netflix. Social media led to something truly magical and life-changing. I joined everything and said yes to as much as I could. I started doing breathwork, pilates, barre classes and yoga through various online platforms and communities. I followed anyone who inspired me and positively influenced me to live life more intentionally and confidently during the pandemic while living alone. I needed something to look forward to every day. The external factors of happiness I had pre-pandemic were no longer available.

In February of 2021, I started an online friendship with a beautiful human who had recently joined something called the Wake Up Call. Since I was saying yes to everything, I said yes to joining this crazy community of individuals who intentionally chose to get up at five every morning to read and talk about personal development.

I was full of energy and optimistic after the first call. I felt a genuine sense of belonging and love for myself. I knew I was where I needed to be. I was already looking forward to jumping out of bed at 5 a.m. going forward.

My first week

During my first week, another member, Silvio, shared his beautiful and enlightening essay titled, "I AM." Listening to Silvio read and reflecting on his essay was the day I had one of those "aha" moments referred to by Oprah Winfrey. Okay, let's be real! I have these "aha" moments almost every day.

Silvio writes, "If the current I AM does not serve you, choose another." All of my I AM's didn't serve me. I told myself, "I am not worthy of love, I will not have a child, or I will not make enough money to buy my own home."

I understood that whatever follows I AM will be my reality, and is a valid declaration of who I will be. Before the Wake Up Call, my actions matched the thoughts I was having, leaving me feeling anxious and depressed. I was constantly worrying about the future or analyzing the past.

My awareness shifted after reading Silvio's essay. I have learned to live in the present moment, the here and now. I learned to tune into the frequency of love every day moving forward. I needed to love myself first. Believing that I loved myself and taking action was the most significant quantum leap I have ever taken when looking within.

Daily affirmations, a gratitude journal, studying, meditation and yoga have become integral to my everyday life. "We become what we think about; energy flows where attention goes," Rhonda Byrnes, author of *The Secret*, reminds us.

Since joining the Wake Up Call in February 2021, my perspective and frequency have shifted significantly. My energy now vibrates at a new level of love and light. I am awake, living each moment with gratitude and love.

I love the growth within myself that I can now project to others. The universe wouldn't give me what I wanted and deserved until I appreciated, became aware, and showed gratitude for all I already had and the moments and experiences that led me to where I am.

Today

I proudly live my life at my pace, mindfully, and intentionally. I trust the universe's rhythm and know I am right where I need to be. I know I will get to where I need to go and have all the time because what I seek is seeking me.

I have learned that the only things in my life that will grow are those to which I give energy, and I am aware that there is a solution for every obstacle. Newton's Law states, "For every action, there is an equal and opposite reaction."

Every day I ride the waves and enjoy the flow of life. I know that with every up, there will be a down. The Law of Polarity tells us that there is an equal and opposite good to everything. The tides aren't happening to us; they are happening for us. I will honour each of these waves and think about what the universe might be trying to teach me. What can I be grateful for at this moment to keep me on the frequency of love?

I am so happy and grateful now that I am in love with who I am becoming and what I am attracting. We don't get what we want; we get what we are in harmony with! I am in harmony with the good. I trust that the rest will follow.

Pep Talk

The Law of Relativity states that nothing is big or small until you relate it to something else. When we compare our lives to someone else's, we set up the thinking that causes us to move into a negative vibration. Nothing is good or bad except that our thinking makes it so. We must learn to stop comparing ourselves to others. Often, we're comparing our lives to the illusion of what is on the surface. We compare our day three to someone else's day three hundred. We see the victory but none of the adversities and failures that were necessary in succeeding. We see someone who seems to have it all figured out, while in reality, they are struggling just as we are.

The Law of Vibration and Attraction, says that you can only attract what you are. The law doesn't know what you want, it only knows what you're in vibrational harmony with. If you are grateful for things as though you already have them, then you can't be left wanting them. You can't want what you already have.

Energy is never created or destroyed, it only changes forms. If you have the image of the thing you want, then you already have it. It's just in its invisible form. There are laws and processes that will move the invisible to the physical if you work in harmony with these laws. For example, wanting sets up resistance and moves things away from you according to The Law of Non-Resistance. When you are grateful for the thing you want as if you already have it, you are working in harmony with the law.

Affirmations

When creating affirmations, create them in the now instead of the future. Kristina wrote: "I am so happy and grateful now that I am in love with who I am becoming." Instead say: "I am so happy and grateful now that I am in love with who I am." Having it now is more powerful than still working toward it.

"You have been criticizing yourself for years, and it hasn't worked. Try approving of yourself and see what happens."

— Louise L. Hay.

Now I vibrate higher

By Elizabeth Rapagna

Today, the sun rose at 5:54 a.m. I was there. I love my morning jaunts to watch the sunrise over Lake Ontario. I love listening to the birds and the water lapping the rocks. The view is spectacular. I always say a prayer as the sun peeks over the horizon. I ask the universe—God, to protect me and keep me healthy. I ask the same for those I love and those I don't know. And I'm grateful for all my blessings. Then I walk along the lake's shore, making my way into town, pick up my cappuccino, head back to the lake, sit on a bench, and enjoy the view. I feel energized and have a sense of deep contentment. There is nothing I need. I've got it all.

I am a cancer survivor.

Two years ago, I received a Stage 4 Cancer diagnosis. I didn't know if I would live or die. I was recovering from one surgery and gearing up for HIPEC/Cytoreductive surgery. The surgery would soon clarify my priorities and save my life. My health and wellness were now centre stage.

So today I decided to run up the stairs in the park. I noted that I wasn't out of breath, or my legs hurt. I wasn't feeling uncomfortable.

"You're doing it," I said. "The changes in your life are taking hold. You are in better shape than ever."

And then it hit me like a wave. Wow, you are a cancer survivor and look what you just did—how did I get so lucky? Why was I given a second chance? Why was I allocated more time? Why do young people, mothers, fathers, sisters, brothers, and children not get a second chance? Why me over someone else?"

There are no answers.

So instead of staying in the why, I moved into gratitude. I am grateful, I am well, and I am blessed. I am grateful I can enjoy the present and imagine my future. I can give and feel love. I have the energy to be a good mom, sister, daughter, and friend. I am grateful for my second chance.

My morning was spectacular.

★

I wrote the above piece in May 2021. I was blogging. I was motivated by a keen sense of giving back and wanting to inspire. I had a mindset of resiliency. I had kicked cancer's butt. I was getting things done but on a subconscious level. I was making changes, bettering myself through healthy eating, exercise, a peaceful environment, and a positive mental attitude.

But with change comes resistance from those who knew me a certain way. This "new me" wanted to see and do more. I even resisted myself. But this me wanted to accomplish big goals and dreams, create an online business, and be financially abundant while being of service. This me wanted to be an example to women over 50, that it's never too late to create the life you've always desired, regardless of where you're at financially, physically, and emotionally. You don't have to wait for a wake-up call called cancer.

Post cancer, I had a strong mindset. My self-image was improving. I was in excellent health. I was involved in social activities, friends, family, and even dating. I had a "say yes" to life attitude. But I wanted more. Way more.

Financially I was in a bad place. My business, The Lizzie Experience, wasn't getting the attention it deserved. I hoped to inspire women through my life experiences from my business, but I had deep-rooted paradigms limiting my success. I wanted to hold myself to a higher standard.

The Wake Up Call

In November 2021, I joined the Wake Up Call. The Call is an early morning community of like-minded individuals seeking an increase in their lives and for those around them. It's about making time to make a difference. Every day, they remind me there are universal laws at play. Once you know how to utilize them, you can accomplish anything.

Imagine starting your day with an inspirational quote or video. You already feel good about yourself for having the discipline to get up early and participate. It's the first win of the day. You surround yourself with a team of individuals who have your back, share wins, and offer encouragement—knowing that you are creating momentum to accomplish your goals by liaising with this awe-inspiring community. People on the Call are genuinely interested in seeing you reach the pinnacle of success. Knowing that you are learning about and practicing universal laws will propel you toward your dreams.

Joe Trimboli is the founder of the Wake Up Call. He saw a positive change in his life by following specific universal laws, and he felt compelled to share how using our emotions as a compass helps us vibrate higher. Our emotions are part of who we are. I choose to learn what I can from my feelings and use my emotions to guide me.

Mindful intentions

Today, my goal in life is to live with mindful intention. Saying "yes" to opportunities, adventures, and experiences. Not being afraid to put myself out there. To be authentic. To be kind. To be of service. To be the very best version of myself. To be gentle and to love fiercely.

The Law of Polarity states that you can't have highs without lows. So, Joe once asked me if I thought cancer was a blessing. My answer is yes. My cancer was a blessing. I embrace this law because I know I wouldn't have the insights without the adversity I have faced.

So why the Wake Up Call? Because I never want to return to being the woman I was pre-cancer. I am determined to continue along the path of self-awareness, self-improvement, and enlightenment. Attending The Call is another strategy in an arsenal of self-actualization exercises that assist me in creating goals and the necessary decisions and actions to attain them—more discipline results in more self-confidence. I am a work in progress. I am aspiring to be the best version of myself. I see myself with health, wealth, and abundance. I'm secure in that vision.

So, who am I?

I am "The Lizzie Experience," and I'm sharing my journey through this crazy, difficult, rewarding, incredible, fabulous, and challenging life. My goal is simple: I want to spread happiness and hope for those struggling through difficulties. I want to share my experiences, wellness strategies, mindfulness exercises, uplifting quotes, affirmations, feel-good stories, and photos. Through my social media presence, events, and writing and speaking opportunities, I am bringing hope to the masses and encouraging women never to quit.

I hope to make a difference in someone's life and be of service the way Joe has made a difference in my life. He has become a mentor. I feel privileged to learn from him. I call him a friend.

I'm still learning, studying, and manifesting my desires with ease, flow, and grace in this incredible, unparalleled community.

I constantly vibrated high; now, I vibrate higher!

Feeling blessed.

Sending blessings.

Pep Talk

We are a mass of energy and energy is always in motion, which means we can never be standing still. We're either growing or we're dying!

As we grow, we may grow apart from some people in our lives while attracting others. It is not an indication that any one person is better than the other but confirmation of cause and effect and of the Law of Vibration and Attraction; like attracts like.

Starting your day right

If you wake up late, stub your toe or spill your coffee, you can expect the rest of the day to follow in much the same way. If you begin your day on a positive note, feeling good about yourself, feeding your mind with information to support good thinking for the day ahead, you set the intention and begin living into a more desirable future. It is always a choice.

Lizzie is already making a difference in so many lives. She uses the morning call as a tool to keep herself focused on her goals, so she can continue to inspire others. When you discover something this good, you can't help but want to share it with everyone, and as you do, you find your special way of expressing this information.

"In the absence of clearly-defined goals, we become
strangely loyal to performing daily trivia until
ultimately we become enslaved by it."

— Robert A. Heinlein.

Creating. Attracting. Becoming.

By Marie-Ann Falcone

I'm zinging with excitement! Being part of this collaboration as a co-author is a notch on my belt, one I would never have thought possible. If you told me I'd be an author, I'd have thought you were crazy. Well? Ta-da! I co-authored *Your Wake Up Call* with many wonderful, talented, and genuine people.

How did I get here?

My life has always been average. I did what society told me to do: go to school, get good grades, go to university, get a job, work, get married, have kids, etc. Well, I had a slight problem. I didn't know what I wanted to do for the rest of my life, nor did I know my life's purpose. I felt lost, ungrounded, and living on autopilot. Going through the motions and hoping something would happen isn't how I wanted to live my life, but it was how I was living—no good habits, no personal development, coasting.

I'd get pissed when opportunities would fall through. Who wouldn't, right? Reacting to every failure and let down as if it were the end of the world until another opportunity would appear.

On the other hand, when I was in harmony with something (when the opportunity felt right), things would magically appear. It would be effortless. I didn't know why I'd struggle so much in some cases and how I'd easily gain all I wanted in other cases. I'd shrug and move on without any awareness about what had happened or how I did it, so I'd have no chance at repeating the process. And my ego got in the way and affected my relationships. Guess when I got rid of my ego. When I got married? Nope. When I had my kids? No, again. Maybe when our youngest was diagnosed with a rare genetic disorder? Warmer. When I joined the Wake Up Call? Bingo! The early morning call is a safe place where people gather to explore personal growth through readings and study.

Before I joined, I always felt offended by what people said to me, and I would react. I took what the person said so personally. That was my ego. When speaking with others, I'd push my opinions on them and expect them to agree. I would judge what I didn't know. My ego needed to be correct, and when it wasn't, I would be annoyed. My ego deepened my victim mentality.

Becoming a first-time mom was the day I felt I knew my life's purpose—taking care of a little human. It was scary, but I loved every minute. It was the first time I had someone more vulnerable than me to care for, so I needed to shake the victim mentality and control my ego. I did, a little. It wasn't until my youngest was born and diagnosed with a rare genetic disorder called Tuberous Sclerosis Complex (TSC) that a little more of my ego chipped away.

I was in a fog. I didn't know about TSC, or how it would turn our lives inside out. What did this mean for our child? I had a choice to make—does this make me bitter or better? It made me a better person. In hindsight, this life event happened for me. Once again, people came into our lives to assist us in providing the best possible care for her. I knew we could focus on providing her with the best quality of life.

Looking into the mirror

Fast forward to the day, I looked in the mirror and didn't know who I was. That day I felt like a hollow shell of my former self, a woman who was faking her happiness and heading in a downward spiral. This spiral kept sucking in negativity, resentfulness, unhappiness, and anger. This woman contemplated walking away from her whole family to start a new life because she thought they would be better without her. The legacy I wanted to leave my kids wasn't consistent with who I was. It was to be a mom, full of love and compassion who wouldn't give up on herself or her family. These feelings went on for years.

Then my youngest was diagnosed with autism, global delay, and nonverbal communication. We dealt with autism meltdowns, strict routines, and finding our normal. Autism meltdowns differ from the usual childhood tantrum. These meltdowns result from sensory overload and the child's inability to self-regulate. My child couldn't verbally tell us what was bothering her. Instead, she'd scream, cry, and grunt.

Having the diagnosis of autism meant our routines were strict. I became isolated and lonely, because of how limiting it would be to go out with her. On top of this, I had to create our new normal (I hate using the word normal, but it seems fitting here). I felt like a failure. I was still reacting to situations instead of responding because I was depleting myself of well-needed self-care to replenish my soul.

One day, I got fed up with this downward spiral. I was a loving and doting mom. I could never leave my family. I could choose happiness, joy, and contentment.

When you are ready: three principles

When you are ready, the teacher will appear. Cue the Wake Up Call.

Living in my comfort zone and not reading, I wasn't growing. Truthfully, I thought, what the hell do I have to lose? I wanted personal development and time for myself. When Joe Trimboli, founder of the Wake Up Call, would explain some principles behind our readings, I spiralled upward. Here are the three principles I've appreciated in my life.

First, everything you want is already here, therefore whatever you want is already here.

I felt a sense of surrender, releasing the notion of chasing my vision or goal. I still have to take action towards my goals. I needed to think about them, and my thoughts became a feeling. I do what I must to get what I want. For example, we attract a clientele that appreciates our value and entrusts my husband to design and build homes.

A second principle that has helped turn my life around is that everything just is!

This principle gives me a sense of calm and peace. It reminds me we can't control everything. This one phrase has helped me respond to external situations with love and understanding.

Another principle, the third, is not being hung up on my "how." How am I going to do that? How can this happen? How. How. How? Forget about it. Don't worry about your how if your vision and passion is strong. This worry would stop me from taking chances in life. I knew I was missing out. No more!

These three principles have liberated me to a life of endless opportunity. I no longer surrender to the old limiting mindset that has held me back. I'm excited to sprint forward with profound hope and faith toward the unknown.

The words, I can't or how, no longer exist. If I want something, I can have it.

Today, my husband is getting calls from potential clients that value his expertise, skills, and knowledge. My oldest is laser-focused on her future with unwavering faith. My youngest has developed and grown so much that she rarely has an autism meltdown, plus her routines don't restrict us as much. There are endless possibilities in my future. I can have anything I desire.

The Wake Up Call has an incredible group of people to start my day and set my mindset right. It holds me accountable to be the best version of myself by putting the principles into action and setting an example for my children. I am on the path of personal growth without guilt and fear. I'm on a higher vibration, so I attract what I want. I've received tools to create a person and a life where I can say, holy crap, who is this person?

Pep Talk

If you want the results in your life to get better, focus on you! As you get better, everyone and everything in your life will get better.

Too often, especially a mom, will weather herself down to nothing but a shell of the person she used to be, eventually giving a lot more than she's capable of and is not able to help in the productive ways she wants to.

We tend to worry and fuss and lose our cool while trying to help, and if you think about it, you'll realize we're not much help to anyone in that state.

When you focus on yourself and your growth and develop an understanding, you become much better equipped to be the person others need for them to improve.

This is all about cause and effect. As we stop treating symptoms and get to the cause more often, we'll see everything in our lives improve.

"Everything in your life gets better when you get better, and nothing is ever going to get better until you get better."

— Larry Winget.

You are one decision away

By Roman Mamalyga

It's a beautiful sunny Thursday afternoon in the picturesque town of Niagara-on-the -Lake. I have my 5 p.m. tee-off time set for our men's night at the local golf club. It's 3:15 p.m., and I'm on my way to the liquor store to pick up a small bottle of vodka and a small whiskey for the after "fun."

Life is good, or so it seems.

But I was tired, hungover, frustrated, and stuck in a downward spiral, living from Thursday afternoon to Sunday night on a bender. I was a functioning alcoholic.

Like most stuck people, I did the same thing repeatedly and expected different results. My old habits, paradigms, and beliefs that weren't even mine had control over me.

I was living the life of an imposter. I appeared great on the outside, but inside I felt like crap. I was always chasing the next shiny object, the next course, the next self-help guru who would have the answer. I lived in doubt, anxiety, and fear and masked it with alcohol. I resigned that this was it, and the booze made it okay.

And so it went as it had gone for 45 plus years until June of 2020.

We were at Sherwood Inn in Muskoka, and I left the suite to go down to the main dining room at 5:00 a.m. to get on a call with 30 people, something called the Wake Up Call led and facilitated by Joe

Trimboli. Little did I know that this man, his vision, and his passion would change my life.

There must be another way

I thought I knew it all. I had studied personal development with the best of them. All the gurus told me that I had to change my behaviour to change results.

The Wake Up Call has taught me that I must change my thinking to change my results. I was focusing on the symptoms instead of the causes. Joe has said that my thoughts cause my feelings, and my feelings (or vibration) create actions that lead to my results.

The tiredness, sloppiness, and overall malaise continued into June, July, and August. In September, I got on a Pep Talk (a weekly call where members can volunteer to take the hot seat and receive coaching) and opened up to 50 people about my life; a life unfulfilled, of broken promises and dreams gone by the wayside. With this, I took a deep dive into my life, and on October 11th I decided to stop drinking.

As I write this, it has been almost 20 months since I stopped drinking. After 45 years of "bingeing," I simply changed my thinking about this part of my life, and it has changed my life.

It is not a habit anymore; it's a standard.

I have raised my standards.

My mental gym

The Wake Up Call has become my mental gym. Every morning I need to get my mental workout. I realize that it is not the goal but the person I am becoming. I am more focused, have more clarity, and use my higher faculties. I can see where I am going.

In December 2020, I took another giant leap. I started studying with Joe as my coach and facilitator of Bob Proctor's legendary personal development and mind study course, Thinking Into Results. Joe's unique style and never-ending insights, experiences, and support have been a rock during the storms of life.

The greatest gift from the Wake-up Call was my wife joining over a year ago. She has grown in heart and soul. Unfortunately, we experienced a personal tragedy last year. I know that the love and support of our Wake-up Call family were instrumental in helping her through the periods of grieving.

I believe God has given me the talent and abilities to teach, lead, motivate, and inspire people. I have been born again. I have more wisdom, knowledge, and experience. All this from a man who was watching the world go by in a bottle two years ago and couldn't wait for the next drink.

I would not be where I am today without the Wake Up Call. I would not have done and had that new standard without the help, love, and support of first my wife, Cheryl, and the foundation set by Joe and The Call family. I see the future as unlimited.

I encourage anyone reading this to reach out to any of us to find out more. You are only ONE decision away from a completely different life.

Pep Talk

"You never change things by fighting the existing reality. To change something, build a new model that makes the existing model obsolete." — Buckminster Fuller.

Roman had to consciously create a new model of who he wanted to be, and by thinking of this model as the new standard, Roman was able to install a new program in his subconscious mind. It is not something that happens just because you become aware of what you want. If that were so, everyone would eat right, go to the gym and drink plenty of water. It happens only after you make a committed decision for a new reality and then, by repetition, install the new program into your subconscious mind.

There is another way—repetition

Many people misunderstand personal growth and development, mostly because they don't take the time to really study it. I watched the movie *The Secret* on a friend's recommendation when I was still struggling, and it upset me. I couldn't buy into what they were saying in the movie because of where I was with my thinking and my level of awareness at the time. After investing all of ninety minutes watching it, I became an expert, telling everyone how ridiculous those concepts were. Stripping anyone I met of any benefit they could have received by following those principles. Going to the odd workshop, watching the odd movie, or reading a book every now and then isn't going to cause any relevant changes. Studying every day, being reminded of things you already forgot a month ago, hearing things for the hundredth time that wouldn't have meant anything to you the second time you heard it, is what equips you with the understanding necessary to make any real, permanent changes. I liken it to going to the gym every day versus going to a boot camp once or twice a year. Boot camps can be incredible for those who work out regularly but can cause a lot of pain without much growth for someone who doesn't. But, if you go to the gym everyday, you get stronger, healthier, and maintain that level of physical fitness. It's the same way for the mind.

Roman's growth has inspired many people and he will continue to inspire and mentor many who are fighting battles he's already conquered.

"The secret of change is to focus all of your energy not on fighting the old, but on building the new."

— Socrates.

Seek and you shall find

By Ashley Spizzirri

Growing up, I never considered myself an anxious person. I was able to make quick decisions, right or wrong, and I never stressed over things out of my control. I was a glass-half-full kind of person with a positive attitude towards life.

Things became heavier into adulthood. In 2015, after the birth of my second child and mobility changing surgery on my dominant hand six months later, I didn't recognize myself. For the next two years, I suffered from crippling anxiety. I was experiencing frequent panic attacks and obsessed over every twitch or spasm in my body.

A practitioner recommended talking to someone, so I invested in a life coach.

Those few sessions were pivotal in my personal development. One session would lead to another, and I started attending weekly meditation classes until I practiced daily. I had more awareness of myself, and how to handle my emotions.

The Wake Up Call

When I joined The Wake Up Call, what I heard wasn't foreign. I had already learned some of these concepts. No one told me about my self-image or learning how to cope with anxiety. I had never heard anything about self-image, but I knew mine was poor.

I had lots of friends and confidence in speaking to people and had no problem in new environments, but my self-image was terrible regarding my weight. I would drop weight and regain weight. I had always struggled in that area. I was so hard on myself and I was exhausted. I remember having a moment with myself in the car where I accepted my body but not in a healthy way. It has felt like an uphill battle my whole life, and now after having kids, years of crippling anxiety, and with my dominant hand having changed forever, I gave up.

When I was 14, I believed I would be happy losing weight. I felt like I was starting on Monday, every Monday. How could anyone develop a healthy self-image?

But when I heard Joe Trimboli, the facilitator of the Wake Up Call, say, "What you are seeking is seeking you," I began to connect the dots. The Wake Up Call is hands down the most magnificent universal magic I have ever experienced, and in divine timing. Let me explain.

In February 2021, one year into the COVID-19 pandemic, I worked incredibly hard to maintain my mental health for everyone around me. I was grateful I had learned how to manage anxiety. My family and I were at my parent's house when my dad, a prominent realtor in the Greater Toronto Area for 35 plus years, received a phone call. We secretly planned a drive-by birthday for him because he would turn 70 the following week. He answered on speakerphone.

The voice on the other end said, "Uh hi, my name is so and so. I saw your story in the Bob Proctor seminar, *You Were Born Rich*, and your story inspired me. I Googled you and saw you are still alive and working. I've been trying to find the courage to call you for two weeks." The man was calling from North Carolina.

What was this guy talking about? I turned to my mom, who was washing dishes, and her reply was, "Oh, he gets seven or eight phone calls like this a year from all over the world." I was stunned. All these years and they never talked about this? In some ways, it wasn't that much of a surprise because my mom had been the one giving me spiritual and personal development books to read. I knew as much as my parents did about Bob Proctor seminars when I was young. I met the man a few times at their Remax office when he held meetings for them. I didn't know my dad participated in the 1986 worldwide seminar. We chatted about it, and he said he had the tapes in the basement. I let it go for the moment.

I couldn't sleep that night. I left the bed, made a coffee, and grabbed my computer. I went straight to YouTube. In my first search, the seminar *You Were Born Rich* appeared. I started scrubbing through and found all the parts where my parents appeared. My mouth hit the floor when I heard my dad speak and say how he had increased his income. I recognized that the two young faces on the screen were my parents.

Is this what they were doing when I was four—mastering their mindsets in business and life? Back then, there wasn't even a self-help section in the bookstore, and my parents were attending seminars. I had a whole new perception of my life as I had known it. I decided it was probably a good idea to watch the entire thing so I could see what it was they were learning. I watched the whole tape that day.

Something was soothing in Bob's voice, probably because I had listened to it in the back of dad's Buick Park Avenue as a kid. I learned about the stick person and the self-image from listening to that 1986 seminar.

The four agreements

The next day I saw an old friend's post that she was part of an early morning book club, and they were reading *The Four Agreements* by Don Miguel Ruiz, the first book someone recommended I read after my surgery. I commented, stating what an excellent book it was. We chatted, and I asked her about The Wake Up Call group.

She said it was open to anyone and that I could join. She was going to send Joe Trimboli, The Call's founder, a message about me. One hour later, I received a welcome email from Joe. I felt pumped, I had always been an early bird, and being home all the time, this seemed like the community I needed in my life. The following morning, I set my alarm for 5 a.m.

The group read for the first part of the Call, and then Joe broke down the reading. I was triggered when he talked about universal laws and the subconscious mind. It sounded like what I heard the day before, watching that 1986 seminar with my parents. It must have been a coincidence, but it was like a punch in the gut when Joe drew the proverbial stick person.

What are the chances?

I felt gobsmacked! I sat in the dark for a while after. What are the chances I learned about my parents in a Bob Proctor seminar from the 80s, and then I join a call where the guy hosting is saying the same things as Bob? Is it a coincidence? No, it is not a coincidence! I felt it was meant to be. The synchronicity behind it was timely.

I kept showing up, and after day four, I had to reach out to Joe. I was so excited to share these new revelations. Joe's response confirmed that this was no coincidence and that the universe guided me.

The longer I participated, the more I resonated with the material. I knew that I was where I needed to be and was eager to learn everything. I showed up every day, took notes, and played full out. I committed to daily affirmations and writing out gratitudes. After a few weeks, I remember telling my mom that I had gained awareness of how I had been talking to myself over the years. Although I have experienced some traumas in my life, I can't let my thoughts run wild.

I felt good about how I was now managing stress and realized I had programmed myself this way, and now was equipped to write a new program. Self-image is everyone's control station, and I knew I had everything mixed up. I promised myself I would never say or think those things about myself again. It is a significant growth area for me, because learning to love parts of yourself you previously hated is hard work. I later realized it didn't have to be so hard.

The commitments to myself are non-negotiable and I hold my image in my mind. I no longer see my body limitations, even with my wrist, because I know my mind can create the environment needed to remain strong. I work with amazing physio-trainers and modify things when needed. I reach personal bests every week.

I have the tools to think my way out of all situations.

Pep Talk

According to Dr. Fred Luskin of Stanford University, we have approximately 60,000 thoughts per day—and 90% of these are repetitive. That means 54,000 of them are the same thoughts we had yesterday! Now, remember that it's our paradigm that controls our habitual behaviour, including how we think.

We will never succeed at stopping these thoughts or preventing the negative ones from entering our minds, but we can begin forming the habit of rejecting or ignoring the negative thoughts and choosing more positive ones. The thoughts that come into our conscious minds are not really a threat if we don't allow them to be planted in our subconscious minds. The awareness of our thoughts is so important. Our subconscious mind is like the earth! Be careful what you plant.

When a negative thought comes, you can choose a different thought in your conscious mind. As you continue to do this, everything begins to improve. I'll go back to the garden metaphor on this one. You won't ever succeed at removing all the weeds and preventing them from returning. Weeds will always grow in your garden, just like negative thoughts will always flash across the screen of your mind. The best action we can take if we want a nice, thick, lush, green lawn is to remove as many weeds as possible and continually overseed with our seed of choice. As more of the desired seeds take root, they begin to crowd out the weeds and leave less room for them to grow.

Ashley became aware of her ability to overseed her mind with the desired thoughts by practicing gratitude, affirmations and adopting a positive mindset on whatever physical limitations have been challenging her all this time. As a result, she's enjoying more positive results in her life and, best of all, peace of mind.

"The mind is a fertile garden—it will grow anything you wish to plant—beautiful flowers or weeds. And it is with successful, healthy thoughts or negative ones that will, like weeds, strangle and crowd the others. Do not allow negative thoughts to enter your mind, for they are the weeds that strangle confidence."

— Bruce Lee.

Life happens for us

By Diana Shalforoshzadeh

The Wake Up Call was one of many opportunities that fell from the sky at the most perfect time in my life. The world had changed. One would think that being locked up in your home you'd meet fewer people. Wrong! I met the most brilliant, like-minded friends, who opened my mind to a world of possibilities.

I was always driven and motivated to better myself, but I often looked for external factors to enhance my happiness. It caused many painful disappointments and unnecessary hardships. I believed that if I didn't struggle and exhaust myself to the brink of burnout, I could not succeed in business, relationships, and fitness.

I am a proud owner of a family real estate team. Our business and industry can be stressful, fast-paced, and unpredictable. I've experienced doubt, worry, and fear, even contemplating quitting.

My relationship with myself was mediocre, toxic, and unhealthy. My views on how to grow my business and relationships felt like an uphill battle with multiple obstacles. As a result, life became complicated and exhausting. Although I was surviving, I wasn't thriving. I never understood why I lived with this lump in my throat and felt emptiness, confusion, irritation, and lack of fulfillment and concentration. It led to anxiety, anger, frustration, and unworthiness.

But I was great at keeping my plate full; busy being busy, one distraction after another. I was becoming reactive and resentful. So keeping my plate full prevented me from flying off the handle.

I began my journey with the Wake Up Call. It caused me to become aware of my many blocks and limiting beliefs. I heard things I'd never heard and was in awe that people on the call shared such deeply personal experiences.

Everything is already here

The Wake Up Call showed me to be aware of my limiting beliefs. The first thing I learned was, "Everything is already here; just forget the how," and soon after, "Resentment is like drinking poison," and more, "Forgiveness is for you, not the other person." These phrases are the most significant gifts I've ever received. They showed me that holding on to my past hinders my personal and professional success, blocking happiness and joy.

Unlike in the past, these phrases became a lingering voice that wouldn't disappear. How could I hide behind my work and other distractions? It was time to grow the hell up!

I began writing gratitude, affirmations, goals, and serenity exercises to help with my reactive tendencies, and committed to showing up and participating in my morning calls. You know what? My energy shifted, and people in my life noticed. I could feel myself heal inside. It was inspiring and gave me a sense of freedom.

Life happens for us

Imagine that freedom begins when we make ourselves responsible for our feelings. Well, I learned the place I needed to start was in forgiveness. I understood I was holding on to a past that was not serving me. As an example, I permitted people and past events the power to reduce me to anger and resentment.

The hardest part was forgiving myself. I learnt that forgiving everything and everyone, our mistakes, our past, and ourselves, leads to the gift of gratitude. When you forgive, you release something, and the magic begins by replacing that space with gratitude. I used to think about certain situations and traumas in the past, and I would physically feel sick. Today, I feel a sense of fullness about forgiving the past, as if something cleansed my heart. A simple shift from life happens TO us, to life happens FOR us, can be the change in perspective that makes forgiveness possible.

Living from the inside out

If I was born perfect, I'd have nothing to work on and life would be monotonous and meaningless. The quest to be better puts me on an exciting journey, and as I continue to grow I realize that I will never be perfect; I will always just be getting better. Working on you is the best project because you can work on yourself for the rest of your life. Knowing you will never arrive at perfection means infinite growth, and there's no ceiling on what you can accomplish.

I began to live from the inside out; my life, business, relationships, investments, confidence, and level of happiness shifted for the better. As I got better, everything around me got better. I attracted things I always wanted with zero resistance. And I felt compelled and responsible for sharing this information with my team and everyone around me. I knew we would see a quantum leap in the business if I could relay a fraction of what I've learned. It worked.

My team felt happiness, joy, success, and gratitude. So, the practice that became a sacred ritual was celebrating wins and gratitude.

When I learned about practicing wins, I did not know what that meant. I had convinced myself that until we hit big wins, we should not celebrate small ones because we don't deserve it. The team practices wins every morning. As a result, we work harmoniously, connect more, and are more productive, driven, creative, and closer.

I dreamt of a day when I could work remotely from a hot climate while my Toronto business thrived. I did not know how, but I didn't let the "how" stop me.

Fast-forward to the end of 2021, when I have made more investments, moved partially to Florida, and am working to have a second base for myself and my team. When you shift your paradigm, it's amazing to see how quickly you shift your results.

My goals are bigger and more audacious than before. My dreams of a massive real estate portfolio rise as my team grows. To get financial freedom from something I love while helping others is a gift I will not take for granted. I remain grateful for all I have now and in the future.

Pep Talk

You may have heard the story of the professor who stood at the front of the classroom, holding a glass of water in her hand asking, "How heavy is this glass of water?" She got all kinds of answers ranging from a couple of ounces to a couple of pounds. Then she asked, "What if I hold it for a minute? What about 10 minutes? What if I hold it for an hour straight? Its weight might begin to make my arm ache a little. But what if I hold it all day? My arm will hurt, and feel completely numb and paralyzed, eventually forcing me to drop the glass. In each case, the weight of the glass doesn't change, but the longer I hold it, the heavier it feels to me."

Everyone has problems in their lives, and to each of us, our problems are the biggest. It's not what we've been through that's the problem, it's that we hold on to it and for how long.

When you gain an understanding and change your perspective, you can let go of what you've been holding onto, thereby making room for new, better things to move into your life!

Our lives are full of what we don't want. To make room for what we want, we have to evoke the Law of Vacuum and clear space for what's to come! Try getting rid of old clothes from your closet and see how quickly newer, nicer clothes show up.

"Your perspective will either become
your prison or your passport."

— Steven Furtick.

Go as far as you can see

By Sandy Casella

The Wake Up Call is an investment in the mind, a way to begin every day with an outlook that declares, "I can control my results instead of my results controlling me."

The mind has always fascinated me. For example, how can two people who come from similar backgrounds and environments, the same family with the same parents, produce dramatically different results? Why do some people come from extreme hardship and grow up to continue along that path, blaming their upbringing for their results until they leave this world, and others who come from similar hardship change the trajectory of their lives?

The answer to this question lies in the Wake Up Call. We become what we think about!

The Wake Up Call

In November 2020, a friend introduced me to Joe Trimboli, the creator of a morning motivation online group called the Wake Up Call. I decided to try it. I dragged myself out of bed the following morning.

Instantly I was hooked!

No matter what is going on in my life, I never miss a call. I went from waking up every morning and feeling overwhelmed thinking about the day ahead to "Wow, today is a clean slate. I can create anything I want."

I understood my past has no control over my future. Steve Jobs said, "You can't connect the dots looking forward; you can only connect them looking backwards." I didn't understand this until months after joining The Call. Job's statement meant we never know how things will unfold in the future to achieve our goal, but we can look back afterwards, and see how everything happened the way it was supposed to.

My goals

I have always had a goal to be a best selling author, but I thought it was impossible. I thought it was only for other people who had more education and training than me. When I became aware that schooling doesn't make you an author; writing does, I let go of the "how" and set "best selling author" as a goal on my vision board for 2021.

I learned on the Wake Up Call that "how" doesn't matter—decide and "the how" will take care of itself. I decided the time was right. I would write my book.

I knew I wouldn't stay committed without guidance, so I hired a publishing company. I had deadlines to meet, and I joined a group of people writing books. Every morning for two hours, we wrote.

When I finished writing, I submitted the manuscript to my publisher. They created a cover, and the book was in the final editing stages. The publisher began promoting it, and we set a release date. But something didn't sit right. Releasing the book meant possibly hurting people I cared about. The book told the story of my family's experience with a mental health crisis, which meant having to expose personal details of someone else's mental health journey. I decided I would not release it. I informed my publisher I was not proceeding with the book.

It was a tough decision. I had spent two years and a significant amount of money. I questioned whether it was my paradigm trying to stop me. When I realized it wasn't, I made the decision and felt at peace.

I'm already a best seller

While working on my book, I accepted an invitation to contribute to a co-authorship book. I completed my chapter and submitted it. It became an award-winning best seller. By this time, I had forgotten what had been written on my vision board. "Best selling author!"

Although it didn't happen the way I thought it would, that is; by way of the original book I wrote, it happened nonetheless. Connecting the dots backwards, "best selling author" happened by way of a book I hadn't planned on writing when I set the goal. If I hadn't written the (unpublished) book, perhaps I would've declined the invitation to write the book that awarded me with the goal.

That's when I realized we could accomplish anything we want. Make a decision, dream big, don't get attached to the outcome, take action, and the universe will make it happen in whatever form it's supposed to.

Many lessons came out of writing the book I didn't publish. My research gave me a lot of knowledge about mental health. I learned that resources are available to people struggling with an addiction or mental illness, but sadly, it is hard to access them. I keep those resources on hand for people I talk with who open up about something happening in their family. I learned that it's not what happens to us that determines our destiny, it's how we respond to what happens that does. If we respond, we stay in control. It's when we react that could be damaging.

Our mental health crisis

During our mental health crisis, I kept it quiet and didn't open up to many people; it led to other problems years later. The healing began when I talked about what had happened and I could help others. When we went through another mental health crisis a few years later, I was much more open, and we could handle it better.

So although the book was never released, I learned many lessons in writing it. I became a different person; the goal for that book didn't matter; who I became in writing the book did.

There are no coincidences in life. We are where we are because of the choices we've made. The law of cause and effect is always working. We can't avoid the effects of this law, just as we can't avoid the effects of any of the universal laws. I commit to constant study every day because the more I think I know, the more I realize how much I don't know.

Go as far as you can see

A few years ago, I drove in the dark through heavy fog. Although I couldn't see past the end of my car, I could still see the front of my car with every foot I drove. It became a metaphor for me, and I lived with the words: "Go as far as you can see. You'll be able to see farther."

Those words have served me well, and my wish for you is that as you continue on your journey, go as far as you can see, and know that when you get there, you'll be able to see farther.

Pep Talk

We often get stuck on what happened to us. We let the thing that didn't go our way completely take over our lives, and we make an alibi out of it, using it to explain where we're at in life. It's almost as if we're okay with living an unfulfilled life as long as we have a good excuse to justify it.

We are going to fail our way to our goal, coming to a crossroads time and time again. The way we perceive something will determine what direction we take going forward. Keep the right perspective, remain grateful and let go of "how" it's going to happen.

For Sandy, her best selling book was supposed to come by way of the book she didn't publish. Sandy's decision to cancel her book was a difficult one, but she followed her heart and did what she felt was right. Just because a decision hurts, it doesn't mean it's the wrong one. Her book may not have been published, but it wasn't all for nothing. While writing her book, she gained experience in the writing process. She acquired specialized knowledge on mental health while doing research for her book that she would later use to help others. Learning that she could even write a book was an important part of her growth and Sandy needed to grow into a "best selling author."

How many people, instead of finding all the good mentioned above, would have focused on the bad instead? Sandy could easily have played the victim. She could have said, "I wasted a pile of money and two years of my life writing a book that I can't even publish."

She would have received all kinds of sympathy from friends and family for her wrong thinking and that would have enforced her victim mindset, arming her with a great excuse for not having done more. When that happens, we are no longer a "best selling author." We go back to who we were before and accept this "failure" as evidence that we truly are "unlucky," or worse—unworthy.

When the co-authorship opportunity came along, would she have said yes if she was the unlucky, unworthy failed author? Would the opportunity have even shown up?

Get crystal clear on how we become what we think about. You can choose what you're going to focus on and that will determine your attitude. Good attitude = good results. Bad attitude = bad results.

"Attachment constrains our vision so that we are not able to see things from a wider perspective."
—The Dalai Lama.

More to life

By Daniela Panetta

I've always felt there was more to life.

I've lived life from the outside in, running in circles searching for joy and happiness through someone or something, hoping to fit in. It's exhausting and makes one feel like they are not enough, never enough.

You would never know that I am a short woman from my big and loud personality. I felt I was too much for most people, and maybe I should tone it down, be the opposite of who I was. Slowly but surely, through the years, I quieted myself until I was utterly lost. Why can't I be like everyone else? I remember wishing I wasn't so loud.

I didn't realize I was making up stories in my head, creating a poor self-image. Growing up, I always enjoyed being amongst my family and friends. I loved being the centre of attention, but I grew distant and spent more time alone at home. I felt unhappy with my relationships, career, and finances.

My journey begins

I began looking into self-development, which led me to mindset training and the Laws of Attraction, a philosophy proposing that positive thoughts bring positive results into a person's life, while negative thoughts bring negative outcomes. I read many books and attended free online workshops. The little voice in my head was new to me. If you haven't heard that voice, it's because you must learn to practise how to quiet the mind. You can achieve this through meditation and breathwork.

I was quite the over-thinker. Not to say that I don't lose my way some days, but I know how to slow down and focus on the present moment. It is a way of living life from the inside out. I am perfect as I am. I was experiencing unhappiness in my friendships, relationships, and career because I wasn't in the right ones. I didn't fit in because I wasn't putting myself in the right places.

The Secret

My cousin gave me a fantastic book called *The Secret* by Rhonda Byrne. I remember seeing the movie in 2006 when I was 25. I could not wait to take what I learned and apply it to my life.

The excitement didn't last long.

I read *The Secret* in two days—I am committed to learning how to develop my mind, body, and soul. This journey is a lifetime. It isn't easy, but having a supportive community is essential.

After several years, I still felt unsatisfied but eager to learn more. In 2021, I told my girlfriend that I would meet Bob Proctor and become one of his consultants one day. One of his many quotes includes, "Thoughts become things. If you can see it in your mind, you can hold it in your hand."

So, I tried it. In the Spring of 2021, I joined the Wake Up Call hosted by the Call's founder Joe Trimboli. He studies the works of Bob Proctor and is a Proctor consultant.

As part of The Call, we read various books to learn how the mind works, how to exercise the mind and the six intellectual faculties. I thought to myself, "What is this?" I remember learning about the six intellectual faculties of our minds during my years of studies, but I didn't give it much attention.

"When the student is ready, the teacher will appear," said Tao Te Ching. So, I was ready to dive deeper and learn more about how the mind works to control how I feel, what I think, and how I can create what I want.

What is it you want?

Do you ever ask yourself that question? It's not selfish to set goals for yourself. We should never limit ourselves to the possibilities available. Sometimes Joe's delivery would rub me the wrong way, but I learned it was because what he was saying was something that I was lacking. Joe was reminding me that self-discipline was up to me. It's up to me to study so I can create new habits. It's up to me to practice showing up as my best self every day. I show up every morning, ready to be my best.

I love that Joe shows up every week to share his information. He doesn't know this, but he pushes me, sometimes my buttons too. We all need someone brave enough to share information that might seem crazy, but the results are incredible when put into practice.

My journey wasn't an easy one, and even though I can do better some days, I am thankful for the many tools that I have in my back pocket. Every day, I am learning to love myself more, creating a stronger and more confident woman.

I have created many daily habits that move me towards achieving my goals. With this knowledge and awareness that continues to grow daily, I left an eighteen-year career to become a mindset coach, consultant, and co-author.

I did not get the chance to meet Bob Proctor in this life, and I'm not a consultant for him, but I work closely with many people in his community. I am a certified mindset coach and success consultant with Uplevel Lifestyle, founded by my mentor, Dr. Spencer Pool.

I am thankful to the people who have introduced me to these unique communities and opportunities. Being a part of The Call has taught me to trust in the process and let go.

My outlook on life today is that anything is possible. Life is what you think of it! Everything is a thought before it becomes a reality.

I am forever grateful for my family and loved ones. They always support me in all my decisions. They are my biggest fans, and I love them.

I am excited to continue developing my mindset and skills so I can share these incredible tools and teachings that are transforming my life. I will continue to push myself because I know that everything that I could ever want is on the other side of fear.

"Faith and fear demand you believe in something you cannot see. You choose." — Bob Proctor.

Pep Talk

Like many people, Daniela thought she would change when she read *The Secret.* Nothing is going to change simply because you became aware of something. Awareness is only the first step. The next and more important step is planting these ideas into your subconscious mind. More often than not, we don't begin taking action until we build a new belief, a new standard, a new self-image; embodying the principles and ideas we've just become aware of. We can't expect anything to really stick after investing only two days of reading, even with the best material!

It is like deciding you want to plant carrots. You know you want carrots, but nothing happens until you plant the seeds in the earth. Ideas are thought seeds, and the subconscious mind is like the earth. It will return to you whatever you plant in it.

The key is to embody these ideas, through study and repetition, so that our behaviour is consistent with what we want. You consciously decide what you want and who you need to be, and then repeat the command to yourself over and over again until the behaviour becomes automatic.

"The eight laws of learning are explanation, demonstration, imitation, repetition, repetition, repetition, repetition, repetition."

— John Wooden.

One day millionaire

By Cris Gabriel

I declare the year 2021 as my awakening year.

One of the significant contributors to my awakening was Joe Trimboli's early morning Wake Up Call community. It is a safe and non-judgemental space where like-minded individuals support each other through readings and sharing stories.

When I joined The Call, I felt inspired by how many participants showed up every morning to read and study motivational books. Unfortunately, I am not a good reader and don't feel confident reading in a group because of my accent. I rarely volunteer to read.

My first week was incredible. The following week I eagerly set my alarm for 5 a.m., and within a couple of days, I moved it up to 4:45 a.m. I am now motivated every morning, and waking up to start my days with this lovely community has become easy!

I came to love reading personal growth books and became fascinated with all things personal development. I eventually grew more confident and have now become a regular volunteer for reading. I always felt content with what I had. I believed the universe had a plan for me and I trusted in the universe, in terms of personal finances, relationships and health, I felt I must be content with what I have because things happen for a reason. I go with the flow of life and accept whatever the universe offers. My dreams aren't big. I never dream about wealth. I dream about helping people.

Two prominent paradigms controlled my life.

One was a money paradigm, and the other a lack of self-confidence.

My money paradigm

I grew up in poverty, believing that I could never be a millionaire or earn a good income. I thought that because I grew up poor, I would remain poor. My father was always struggling to make ends meet. He didn't have a full-time or regular job. Sometimes he was away for one or two months, working outside our province. There was no definite date for his return.

His coming home was always a surprise and he'd come with a significant amount of cash. He would tie the money with an elastic band and stuff it in a paper bag. We would have a variety of delicious food on the table, new toys, and new dresses for a special occasion or a holiday like Christmas. This happiness and excitement would last only a few days and then the money would vanish like dust in the wind. My father had many habits, including smoking, drinking, and gambling. He would lose the last penny in his pocket through gambling. I called my father a "One Day Millionaire."

My first paradigm—money

My sisters and I had a brief experience of an abundance of delicious foods, candies, chocolate, and ice cream. This experience only lasted for one or two days; the next thing I knew, we were back to zero. No food on the table! No money to pay the bills. I return to living my dream and asking myself when is dad's next millionaire day? My father, throughout my childhood, kept the same habits. His life was like a Ferris wheel, an infinitely large cycle of highs and lows;. the same result he created repeatedly.

I am so grateful to my mother. She's our angel. My mother was the gentlest, most loving, patient, and beautiful person. For the first ten years of my life, I experienced living with this beautiful person. She left us early. She got very sick, and as a child seeing my mother suffer I felt relief when she passed. I know she's no longer feeling the pain and enduring the suffering because God now cares for her.

One memory of my mother is how she would keep or hide money. She hid money between the mattress and box spring and sewn in her dress's seam. She also hid it in the secret pocket of my grandfather's old coat. Because when my father lost all his money from gambling, he would come home with zero money, which meant zero food on the table. When that moment happened my mother would take her money, go to the market, and buy food to cook and feed us.

Becoming the breadwinner

Growing up in this environment caused me to form the habit of worrying about the future. So, at 19, I started working for the Government. I became the family's breadwinner. My father could not work anymore because his health had deteriorated after several strokes and heart attacks. I lived with my father and three siblings at my grandparents' home. The money I made was for food and utilities. I always came up short, but I survived and continued working hard.

I then worked at a manufacturing company and gained experience working overseas. I believed I could earn money from working hard. Saving money for the future is what I do. I spend money on needs and not wants. I want to be practical and spend my money wisely.

Later, I worked in Canada as a babysitter for a Canadian couple. After my contract ended, I worked in a manufacturing company in Newmarket, Ontario and also started a cleaning business. I worked 12 to 14 hours on the weekdays and worked every weekend. But after ten years of doing the same thing and having the same results, I was saving money BUT not enjoying life.

The massive rock drops

One day, the universe dropped a massive rock on me. I got very sick; this sickness led me to choose to live and enjoy life. I quit my job and trained to become a Yoga, Meditation and Reiki teacher and started a business providing wellness services. I transitioned to wellness for myself and wanted to share it with others. But, despite this change, I was not earning enough money.

My second paradigm—a lack of self-confidence

In 2021, I attracted the perfect mentors, community, and programs to shift my paradigms. I knew I needed to change, and I needed support to change my results. Personal growth webinars, the personal development community, and business opportunities were coming simultaneously. I invested in myself and took the Bob Proctor Coaching Program. I know what I want, and I have a big goal.

According to Bob Proctor, repetition is the first law of learning. Repetition alters a paradigm. Studying is essential for changing and creating new habits. I changed my relationship habits with money. I shifted my money paradigm. Sometimes the habits return, but the good news is I have the awareness now. I need to raise my vibration and keep my attitude on track.

Every morning I am reminded and inspired to vibrate high, study, and learn. As I am always reminded on The Call, "You are the highest form of creation," and we live on the three planes of understanding: spiritual, physical and intellectual. We are spiritual beings living in a physical body and have intellect." There is perfection in each of us. It is a beautiful concept.

I shifted my paradigms through studying, gaining knowledge, applying the laws of the universe, and understanding myself.

Studying Bob Proctor's teachings with Joe and having this community for accountability, enhances my growth. My growth journey and realization of my goals will continue with the Wake-Up Call community.

Pep Talk

As I've said before, you cannot outperform your self-image and can never go beyond where you think you can. Money paradigms and insecurities are deeply rooted! We inherited our limitations in our childhood, accepted other people's beliefs, and they became our own. We overheard our parents or caregivers worry and argue about money and expenses. We were told what was right, what was possible, what was wrong, and what we should and shouldn't do.

When you think back and become aware of this, you may find it tempting to blame your parents or guardians. Don't! It's not their fault. They did the best they could with what they knew, from their level of awareness at the time. Just be grateful you're becoming aware of this now.

When you begin questioning your beliefs, you'll see that many of them will fall away. Regardless of your beliefs and the opinion you have of yourself, the ability to be happy and successful in everything you put your mind to is inside you. It's in your DNA... It's just hidden underneath all that virus code, or wrong thinking.

You can clean up those viruses by studying and gaining a better understanding of the laws of thinking and the laws of the universe. As you do that, you'll begin to express more of who you really are. Who you really are, before the limiting beliefs and wrong thinking was programmed into us, is pure unadulterated spirit with unlimited potential.

"Believe, and your belief will create the facts."

—William James.

On the wings of faith

By Nancy Jannetta

I have been travelling through life on the wings of faith and love, which have helped me through tough and dark times. I know that what my mom told me at four was the truth. She always said, *"Your dad will always be there for you, and so will God. You can talk to them—they will answer your prayers and protect you."*

At four, you don't question your mom. I found comfort in the darkness, knowing that my dad, God, and what I know to be my angels were always there. The evidence appeared in remarkable ways and strengthened my faith. I also learned life wasn't perfect. There are many lows and challenges, and I could heal the pain through the energy of love. I believe strongly that faith and love lay the foundation for a life of happiness.

A balanced life

In 2015, at 40, I worked as an early childhood educator in a kindergarten classroom. But after a concussion and treatments for cancer that left me with a disability, I could not work. I prayed for a solution and found a wearable neurotech product called human performance technology. It balanced my brain, provided me with energy, and gave me back my life.

I spent my days dreaming about how I could give back and work with kids again. I also became a Reiki master and worked on my healing using this energy. Further, I went to an event that completely changed my perception of money and investing in myself. I always said, "I don't need money to be happy." Then suddenly, I had an epiphany—with more resources I could contribute to worthy causes and significantly impact my community and the world.

My growth led me to more change. I was learning how to live on purpose, love myself fully, accept where I was, and heal while moving forward and reaching my goals. Now I was 44 and learning I didn't have boundaries. I remember thinking, what do people mean by boundaries?

I learned that boundaries are what we use to teach people how to treat us.

I could see my lack of boundaries was a lack of self-love. I dug further and learned about my core values and other life-changing concepts. It was one aha moment after another. Nancy, it's time to step up.

Pandemic halt

However, everything came to a halt during the COVID-19 pandemic. It shut down my business activities. I felt a little relieved. I was tired, so I turned inward and prayed. What appeared into my awareness, and had been there all along, was an opportunity instead of a catastrophe. It gave me a space to grow and learn more. I deepened my knowledge and got excited about my new goals to help people heal, thrive, live cleaner, healthier lives, and create wealth. Educating and sharing what I knew about natural tools and healing became my passion and career. I have an immense desire to help others heal their pain, get unstuck and achieve their goals.

Joining the Call

One day, I talked with my friend Michele, and we wondered how we could help kids. We both knew how many children were struggling with mental health and that the numbers were climbing. She asked me if I wanted to join a Wake Up Call, an early morning gathering of like-minded people where you can learn and grow a stronger mindset.

They were reading *Think & Grow Rich* by Napoleon Hill, the next book I was planning on reading. I remember thinking I wanted to wake up at that time because that's what successful people do! So, I said, "Yes." I felt I had manifested this call. I enrolled in Bob Proctor's *Thinking Into Results* (TIR) program and learned how to teach manifestation. The space I was in felt like home.

On day two of The Call, scared as I was, I felt compelled to speak up when Joe Trimboli, the founder and leader of the Wake Up Call, said, "Does anyone have anything they want to say?" As I sat staring, waiting for someone to speak, my brain said, "He needs you to speak up." Shyly, I opened my mouth to share my story of faith and how it took me over seven years to become pregnant. We had just read this story in Wayne Dyer's book, *The Power of Intention*. The events that followed by simply sharing my story further opened my mind to my heart's desire to help more people heal.

Two weeks later, I found out that Joe was a TIR coach. I couldn't believe I had manifested what felt like group coaching five days a week! I saw more miracles; people chasing their dreams and bringing them to fruition.

I knew I had to speak up, stop being afraid, and activate my faith. Every morning I heard, "You gotta start." It replayed in my head. I was learning about the power of spaced repetition and the universal laws, and was eager to learn more and to understand the concepts deeper.

I could feel myself shifting.

My confidence was growing and I finally took steps toward realizing my dreams. So, I created a call for my colleagues to practice success habits. This call took place right after the Wake Up Call. I would journal, meditate, and feel inspired. I would come in full of energy, beaming with inspiration, sharing the morning's lessons. I later opened the business partners' call to everyone. It has developed into Mornings Are For Me!

A call for kids

On the Wake Up Call one morning, we asked, "Why aren't kids taught this? Why wasn't I taught this?" I began dreaming about how I could impact kids. I created a space called Call For Kids, where I help kids to discover their inner superpowers (what Bob Proctor refers to as the higher mental faculties). We discuss struggles and find tools to help. I especially love to teach them to set goals, practice gratitude, learn self-love, and ultimately create their dreams.

My passion for sharing what I was learning grew, and this is when I decided I wanted to help other women remove those limiting beliefs so they could heal, thrive, and live life on purpose with love and faith at their core.

All of this happened fast because I took action, kept my faith, and was willing to serve. It was exciting! I had to dig deep to find the courage to start. While I had so many great mentors supporting me, it wasn't easy. It challenged me every step of the way. What I learned is that, when the challenges show up, breakthroughs happen. When I stepped up to a challenge, circumstances would improve. At times, I was on a great roller coaster ride. There was a consistently exhilarating yet scary feeling that usually stops people in their tracks, and it was also the feeling I knew I had to get used to experiencing; if I wanted to make my dreams a reality, that is.

I see myself speaking to millions and spreading the message of love, self-love, faith, happiness, and relaying the teaching that we are born creators that can manifest our desires. I see myself writing books and building a foundation to help with so many of the struggles faced by children.

I am enjoying life fully and creating the time and financial freedom that will allow me to live out my dreams, to continue serving, creating, and helping as many people heal and thrive as possible, one baby step at a time.

I'm incredibly grateful for my support system—my daughter, family, friends, and every mentor who supported me. I look forward to the future. I'm excited, and I've only just begun!

Pep Talk

Many people who hear this information wonder why this isn't taught in schools! It's rather sad. I remember sitting in class, trying to pay attention. Trying to keep my focus on what the teacher was saying but no matter how hard I tried, I couldn't do it. I was sitting at my desk, the teacher was talking, but I was somewhere else. I was flying with the birds through the sky, just outside the window. My body was at my desk, but I was someplace else.

My dreams would be interrupted by a booming voice. "Joe! Pay attention! Quit looking out the window and listen to what I'm telling you!" and then I'd be called on to stand up and answer a question I didn't know the answer to. I felt bad. I felt stupid. I felt humiliated. I didn't mean to disrespect the teacher. Where was I for the last five minutes?

I was six years old. I didn't understand why I wasn't allowed to use my imagination. Maybe things would've been different had the teacher come over to my desk and gently said, "Joe, tell me where your wonderful imagination has taken you and then I need you to come back to this classroom and use your will to focus on what I'm teaching. You see, your imagination is your superpower that allows you to dream and create, and your will is your superpower that gives you the ability to focus. Whenever you find your mind wandering, bring it back to what you should be paying attention to".

I was 40 years old when I heard my mentor Bob Proctor tell a similar story and I remember pulling over, sitting in my car and breaking down into tears like that six year old would have. Sobbing, heartbroken for that little boy, feeling one of the moments where a little part of me died! I felt a rush of hope sweep into my heart, and I knew then that one day I wanted to teach this to kids.

Nancy and a few other teachers who'd been on The Call have since worked this material into their classrooms, and sometimes they come back and tell us about it on the calls. See, I didn't know how I would do it, but I am indirectly teaching this information to kids. I'm sharing information that teachers take and bring into their classrooms. This is how it works. I didn't need to know how I was going to do it. It's not going to look the way you think it's supposed to look. Oftentimes, it's much better than how you could've imagined it yourself.

"Imagination is everything.
It is the preview of life's coming attractions."
— Albert Einstein.

Endlessly blooming

By France Theriault

November 8th, 2021, was the first day I attended the Wake Up Call. I came to this online gathering because I heard about it from a friend. She eulogistically attributed her progress and wonderful outcomes to this virtual community's daily 5 a.m. attendance.

After my first call, I felt a surge of electric energy vibrating in my body. The words, the essence, tangible vibes, and the community's people were extraordinary. I felt this phenomenal, high vibratory energy in my body for at least three weeks until it became a new normal.

My journey

I was already on an eight-year spiritual and personal growth journey. In 2013, I had a tragic cycling accident that resulted in a traumatic brain injury (TBI), and I embraced my spiritual awakening process. I realized I would need to rely on something bigger than myself in this new life's invitation, so I eagerly started my quest. I was open to learning about myself, and the mystical forces of life.

Inspirational quotes, holistic healing practitioners, self-development books, oracle cards, and many other influences assisted me in reassessing my life and reinventing myself. Journaling, meditating, reciting affirmations, writing about my dreams, and visualizing favourable outcomes were part of my daily routine even before attending The Call. Spending time in nature became a wonderful healing process I have discovered as I learned to slow down and be present with myself, and my environment.

Over the years I became passionate about sharing my healing journey. Being a TBI advocate was a calling I felt honoured to embrace. Eight years later, I am still at home pursuing my healing journey and trying to identify what will bring me joy, and how to be of service to others while making a living.

By 2021 my health was better. I was experiencing physical pains and some cognitive issues, mostly invisible to someone looking or having a conversation with me.

My relationships improved. I already had fabulous friends who were present, caring, and understanding. Welcoming new friends who are vibrating wholeness and inclusiveness is incredible. But my interactions with family members were chaotic and tense.

A work in progress

As for my self-image, I am a work in progress. I am kind, compassionate, curious, audacious, ambitious, caring, and engaging. I am reassessing my worthiness, which leads me to rewrite new scripts about what I deserve.

My first read with The Call was *The Power of Your Subconscious Mind* by Dr. Joseph Murphy. Page after page, I discovered countless insights that validated some of my experiences, and new ones that expanded my mind. I love when Wake Up Call founder Joe Trimboli interjects some teachings or when someone shares their life experiences. These repartees of spiritual concepts, universal laws, and serendipitous moments make me smile.

I finally connected some dots of events, concepts, experiences, and synchronistic events that unfolded magically. I knew it had nothing to do with chance. "Nothing happens by chance. This is a world of law and order," states Dr. Murphy. While reading this, I realized I didn't have the words or knowledge to grasp what was happening or what had happened to me.

You don't get what you want in life, you get what you are in harmony with, was a revelatory catchy phrase I learned from The Call. I understand it more and more every day.

Intentions

One of my favourite quotes from *The Power of Your Subconscious Mind* is, "I make my life greater, grander, nobler and richer."

I knew being intentional was part of favourable outcomes. I understood that being grateful and appreciative are two magnetic elements of abundance and prosperity. Selecting a goal and taking small incremental steps are essential for making our dream a reality. I have done it so many times. One of my attributes led me to overcome many challenges in my recovery journey. After my cycling accident, I experienced many of these concepts without knowing the law of vibration or the law of perpetual transmutation of energy.

Being a student of life with an incessant desire to learn more to attract what I want in life fascinates me, and it's one reason I rise early every morning to attend The Call. I realized late in my adult life that I am 100% responsible for my destiny. I felt paralyzed and unprepared even though I was a well-seasoned adult living solo after having a TBI. But listening to the words read by many of The Call's members' comforts me. They ignite a renewed sense of trust and faith that I am an active participant in writing the script of my desired life. Learning new concepts and repeating similar lessons with different words bring a deeper understanding. Life is a process and changes are inevitable. Giving myself some grace in the transformative process is a beautiful gift.

It is almost impossible to choose one moment that significantly affected my life. I believe it's a continuous stream of micro-moments juxtaposing to make an impact. I admire people's vulnerability, rawness, and generosity as they disclose personal challenges, insights, and events.

I also appreciate it when people openly ask questions for clarifications, or for guidance about a difficult situation. We are all very similar, and our humanness brings us to experience relatable problems.

I am deeply grateful for Joe's vision to create a community of seekers of the Truth who are phenomenal agents of change. His dedication, as well as his impactful contributions are remarkable. Members of this community eagerly deepen their thoughtful explorations, edit their mindsets, and change to become the best version of themselves.

One idea I have invited back into my peripheral vision is focusing on what I want in life instead of its opposite counterpart. This concept creates new scenarios about relationships that need repair. I declare my intentions, write them, and daydream about them.

I envision my future financial situation knowing being prosperous is more than a frivolous idea; it's a reality that is on its way. I see myself being healthy, vibrant, and athletic again. I set my goal of pursuing my dreams of living abroad, writing books, becoming a paid transformational international speaker and having art exhibits worldwide. It's a large command for the universe. I know the universe and I are an exquisite, powerful duo.

Allowing and accepting what is coming my way, knowing everything just "is", it's neither good nor bad, opens my mind, relaying judgements and inviting curiosity to lead the way.

Bringing at the forefront what I want in life and giving energy to this concept brought magical moments I desired for so long. Being patient and letting go of the exact moment to unfold came from studying with this community.

More confidence

Five months later, I am more confident and have gained clarity about my gifts and how to use them. For example, I understand that the words I release into the universe are declarations. More, I observe my thoughts and rapidly notice the sliding hill I'm climbing when negativity, morosity, and melancholy visit. I can choose my thoughts and words again and again until I vibrate higher.

As I venture into new experiences and opportunities, I have a greater idea of who I am. I am optimistic about the unfolding of beautiful events, people, and opportunities on their way.

Where do I see myself in the future?

In various countries, enjoying life and being of service to humanity by doing what I love: writing, painting, taking photos, speaking, sharing the wisdom and insights I gained over the years, and being a creator of beauty.

I desire to live passionately every day and leave behind a legacy. May my life inspire others to live kindly, generously, and lovingly, knowing we are the creators of our reality.

Pep Talk

Someone once said, "The person who loves walking will walk further than the person who loves the destination." France has really learned to enjoy the journey! The more we learn, the more we express ourselves more fully. Spirit is always for expansion and greater expression, and as we allow more of this energy to flow, the more we discover who we truly are.

My mentor would always say, "We are spiritual beings living in a physical body, and we have an intellect." Spirit or energy is limitless! But it resides in this physical body that is limited by the quality of our thoughts. Our thinking is like a governor on this machine we're operating in. It would be like putting a governor on an F1 race car. The fact the car has over 1,000 horsepower doesn't matter if we were to install a governor that limits its power to 100 horsepower.

The car would only be capable of expressing as much power as the governor allows. As we raise our awareness, we raise the quality of our thoughts and as a result, raise the limit on this governor and the results we get in our lives.

"Life is change; growth is optional. Choose wisely."

— Albert Einstein.

Starting to dream again

By Carolyn Maiero

O nce upon a time, there lived this girl. She loved her job as a financial planner, working with people and providing peace of mind and direction. She loved her friends and family, and was very active with golfing, skiing, cycling, hiking and travelling.

Then one day, her life came to a halt. One minute she was walking, and the next, she was staring up at the ceiling, lying in a pool of blood. She blacked out. She had hit her head on a wrought iron door handle, a chair, and the floor. Life took a 180. The damage continued for the next five years—days, months, and years of struggles—light and sound became her enemies. The simplest tasks felt insurmountable, like getting out of bed and brushing her teeth. Everything which had been so easy before, had become a struggle or nearly impossible.

In her journal one day, she wrote:

Who am I?

I look in the mirror, and a stranger looks back.

I don't recognize her.

Who is she?

Why is she here?

Where did I go?

I look back at pictures; it is like I'm looking at someone else's life.

I don't remember that person, that life.

Who am I?

Why am I here?

So that is a bit about me. I was feeling purposeless and hopeless. My life was no longer what it was, and my capacity to do my job and live my life as before was no longer. Anxiety and depression built up as I struggled to find my new normal. My relationships changed. Not everyone understood. I appeared fine on the outside. On the inside, there was so much pain and struggle, but I slowly started on a spiritual journey to figure out who I am. I joined a few support groups for brain injury and have built some beautiful relationships, and things have progressed. Not until Joe Trimboli's Wake Up Call did I realize that my life was just beginning.

Not awake

Before the accident, I was not awake. I was going through life as most of us do; work, play, work, play, and going through the motions of what I was supposed to do—go to school, get a job, get married, have kids, work hard, buy a house, save for retirement, and take some holidays. In reality, life became work, work, work, and some fun in between. The accident brought to light that I had defined myself through my work. When I looked in the mirror, I no longer recognized myself. I didn't have my job anymore, so who was I?

I'd look at pictures of my past life, remembering things. Everything feels like a lifetime ago, each segment of images seemingly a different person. I cannot believe who I was before, possibly because I didn't know. I was drifting, thinking I was living my life. Now I question whether I was merely doing what my program wanted me to do.

My higher faculties

I am learning about my higher faculties, their magnificence, and their infinite possibilities. Nothing is created nor destroyed. I couldn't see it, but I feared my endless possibilities.

For example, I always believed I had a poor memory. One day, Joe corrected me. I have a weak memory, a muscle in my brain that I can build and improve. I once believed some people are more intelligent than others at school—that they were born that way. That's not true. We all have greatness in us!

It is a matter of realizing the universal laws and learning to tap into our six higher faculties of imagination, intuition, memory, perception, reason, and will. I recognize that life is happening for me, not to me. Everything in life is a win or a lesson and nothing else.

Did you know worrying is like praying for what you don't want? Whenever I start down that rabbit hole of worry when something happens, I remind myself of that saying and shut down that worry.

Every morning

I now wake up at 5 a.m. every morning in anticipation. I make my celery juice and settle in with my pencil and pad and whatever motivational book we will read on The Call. I am part of a beautiful community of like-minded people who want to grow.

In the past five months, I have learned so much through the influential books we have read, for example: *The power of your subconscious mind, Change your paradigm, change your life, Wishes fulfilled* and *The strangest secret.*

The most significant impact has come from the community and people being vulnerable and sharing their struggles and dreams.

Hearing from those on The Call and how they have overcome obstacles and achieved success by setting goals and drawing on their higher faculties, shows me that anything is possible.

In my faith, I believe that anything is possible. I am meant to be here, and I am worthy. To live from the inside out, I must respond and not react. I have a choice about what I want to think and believe. Everything is energy. There are frequencies, and I have the power to change the frequency. The importance of gratitude, forgiveness, and giving up on the hope that the past could be different. Happiness is a choice!

Once upon a time

I've always wanted to start a book that way, and now I am doing it.

Who would've thought I would be a co-author, part of a collective of beautiful like-minded people? Six months ago, I sure didn't!

My accident was the beginning of a new journey. Joe's Wake Up Call provides me with the tools to learn and grow. I can dream again.

Life is not over.

It is just the beginning!

Pep Talk

Sometimes, the only way to move forward is to let go of the life you thought you were supposed to live, so you can begin living the life you're meant to live. When you compare a thing to anything else, you are evoking the law of relativity. Nothing is big or small, good or bad until you compare it to something else. When you compare what your life is now to what you think it should or could be, you're moving onto a frequency where you cannot see the life you're meant to live.

We're so attached to things going how we want that we stand in the way of something better!

"Energy is never created or destroyed." When you understand this, you understand that we, as creative beings, can transmute this energy by the way we use our higher mental faculties.

Energy just "is." We make it what it is by the way we think. When our thinking is influenced by the negative comparison, we cause ourselves to move into a negative vibration. When you become aware of these laws, and the power we have to use our mental faculties on purpose, we can begin creating the energy that will manifest into the results we want to achieve.

When Carolyn became aware of this, she started to live into the future that reflects more of who she really is! You are not your job title, position or status. You are the highest form of creation and can always create something new.

> "When I let go of what I am, I become what I might be.
> When I let go of what I have, I receive what I need."
>
> — Lao Tzu.

The shift

By Daljit Dhanjal

When I graduated from university, I worked as an instructor therapist for children with autism. I shared a special connection with them because, although I was there to teach, I was the one who learned many lessons.

Two particular children come to mind, both non-verbal and low-functioning; although they had never spoken to me, their eyes spoke volumes to my soul. It's fascinating to discover the power of our intuitive nature. It caused such a shift in my heart, and I wish I could express how profound their impact was on my life. I knew then that I had to do more than merely work to make money.

I was not qualified to be in a position requiring self-awareness, a sense of responsibility, and a deep understanding of other individuals' needs. I quit my job when I realized that staying in my position was an injustice to the children. That's when I began a profound journey to self-discovery.

Lost and confused

I was lost and confused for years following, jumping from job to job and questioning what was wrong. Why couldn't I settle at a job for longer than a few months to a year? Did I not have what it took? What the heck was wrong with me? It went on for three years. Finally, I left the social services field and started a business, hoping that I would become the woman I need to be first, for myself, others, and the overall fulfilment of my soul's purpose.

It would require a lot of growth. I was ready to embark on that journey. I started my business, experienced difficulties, and faced my demons. I tried to carry myself through, but I needed help.

When the student is ready, the teacher will appear

I saw a post about a motivating morning wake-up call, and I felt attracted to the idea. The Wake Up Call helps you gain the motivation and confidence to thrive by forming healthy habits and a routine you love. So I joined and was on The Call the following morning.

Right away, I learned that being in harmony with an idea and acting on the inspiration or intuitive message you receive, can change the course of your life. I know where I would be today if I had rejected The Wake Up Call and scrolled past. That one decision to join changed my life. It gave me the guidance I needed to start my business, overcome my negative self-talk, connect with a community of like-minded people in a safe space to discuss my struggles, and pursue solutions, encouragement, and empowerment.

One person's story can inspire you to begin the process. I am happy to share some lessons that have made a difference.

First, the shift begins when you decide, with no room for what-ifs or maybes, to move straight into action.

The great motivator, Bob Proctor, says, "Goal setting is an intellectual exercise; goal achieving is a lawful process." Let that sink in. If achieving your goal is a lawful process, aren't you curious to know what that might be, how to get into harmony with all you desire? It is a matter of aligning a few things with the universe's timing.

Second, the Law of Cause and Effect is the law of all laws. The reciprocation of the universe will focus on the cause of what you desire. Simple yet astonishing! One thing to be cautious of, is that this information is not enough. But repetition helps install new habits, beliefs, and paradigms.

It is common to run into many limiting beliefs and internal and external challenges when starting a new business. The most important thing is to hold on to something deep within yourself, which deepens your roots to stand tall when life tests you.

Sometimes, we cannot bear the tests alone, so you must surround yourself with people who believe in you and your capabilities. What caused the most significant shift in my life was taking a moment every day to celebrate a win. It was anything from enjoying coffee with a friend to closing the biggest deal in your career. The little wins lead to the big ones. It builds momentum and keeps you going when you don't feel like doing anything.

Initially, I struggled with deciding what I wanted for almost a year and a half. One day, I set my heart firmly on what I wanted, with no other way out, and things shifted within an hour of making that decision. Boom—a result!

I let go of the "how" or "what ifs," and the universe or God instantly kicked everything into gear and made it all happen. I questioned whether it was a coincidence or luck; however, I knew I was in harmony with my goals as life continued.

It's incredible to see how quickly things shift when you focus on yourself, your goals, and your dreams, with nothing from the external world to influence the picture you've painted on the canvas of your mind. Although negative thoughts and emotions are inevitable, the daily study of this material constantly aids in installing a new program in your mind that aligns more with the person you want to become.

Imagine spending the rest of your life peeling back the layers of who you are and falling deeply in love with yourself. I am blooming into the woman I am meant to become. I am constantly working on my mindset, beliefs, and paradigms, trying to align the inner world with the outer, while surrounding myself with people who hold me accountable and call me out on my bullshit.

The next level

I see myself taking my business to the next level. I'll uncover my soul's purpose more deeply. I'll do work in this world that inspires the next generation to discover the light within, empowering them to embrace their highest potential and live a life according to their values.

Once we embrace our potential, we can step into our power and take on life as a movie that we get to direct. It's beautiful. The negative thoughts will always be there, and life will continue to test us, but it comes down to how you *choose* to think, what you choose to believe, and how you bounce back up after each adversity.

A daily practice of gratitude goes such a long way. Gratitude is not merely an intellectual exercise. When you are grateful, you feel it.

I'd like to express my deepest gratitude to the two children who moved me. You've changed my life. To my family, you've taught me patience. To my niece and nephew, you've awakened the most beautiful part of my soul, and a special type of love that I cannot even begin to describe. To the Wake Up Call community, you've shown me the importance of connectedness when the world isolated itself. And Joe, you've propelled my life five years forward in one year!

With lots of love,

Daljit Dhanjal.

Pep Talk

I love how quick people are to thank others and give others credit for "changing their life!" While I appreciate and graciously receive notes of thanks and praise for changing a person's life, I'm humbled by the knowledge that it's never me! It's never anyone except the person who's doing the work. Imagine if we were all as kind to ourselves as we are to everyone else!

Daljit made a decision and kept choosing, again and again, to show up for herself, no matter how difficult it was and how uncomfortable it became—she was the one doing the work; it was all by her own actions. It's incredibly humbling to witness that in every single case the individual is responsible for changing their lives. She simply became aware of information she hadn't heard before. She gained a different perspective here, took a different approach there, and eventually became aware of the power she already possessed. No one can and no one will ever do it for you! All that the two children did for her, all that her parents did, all that the Wake Up Call did, all that I did, was provide the inspiration or information that gave Daljit cause to change her life.

What I know for sure is that every single person has everything they need to completely change the direction of their life. They just need to take 100% responsibility for everything and become aware of what they don't know they already have!

"Who looks outside, dreams;
who looks inside, awakes."

— Carl Gustav Jung.

You're meant for more

By Michele Steko

"**Y**ou're meant for more, Michele; you're meant for more."

For years that voice replayed in my head. Eventually, everything would change because of it. I just didn't know it. But where was this voice coming from? How can a message be so bold, loud, and clear? Welcome to the Wake Up Call.

Before signing on to the Wake Up Call, my way of living would be familiar and mundane to most people. The comfortable and everyday routines of work, eat, sleep, and repeat was a weekly train that only stopped at weekends.

Learning to wear so many hats over the years and wear them well was becoming exhausting and monotonous. I worked in business development and mortgage sales for many years, pounding the pavement, building relationships, attending events, and networking. I made it look easy. It gave me a lot of flexibility to be the best wife and mother I could be.

But somewhere, I started to think where it was leading me.

For 15 years, I balanced work and family life. I was living on a schedule, a calendar warrior where the essence of time became a commodity. I existed to honour that calendar. Living an arduous structure served its purpose. It kept the train moving.

Still, I was enjoying my roles in business development and management. I had a real thirst for teaching and educating others which was the most rewarding part of my role, even though it came with many other fine perks.

I had what I needed in life. But it hit me one day, waiting at a traffic light, exhausted, looking over at the lifeless, robotic, and miserable looking person in the car next to mine. Life was feeling heavier, and people everywhere around me were growing in their negativity. And everywhere I looked, I could see the dismay and frustration people were living day in and day out. I thought, "This can't be it. There has to be more!" I believed there was more.

I was now on a search, a desperate search for change, something that would help me understand why I was looking for more. That's when the phone call I needed came. The call came from Joe Trimboli, the founder and leader of the morning online call. I felt captivated when he told me, "The biggest problem in the world is ignorance."

Waking up early, very early

On Canada Day, 2020, I committed to waking up early and opening myself up to change. What was I going to learn? I had everything down to a science! Little did I know that life would never be the same and that I was embarking on a journey that, not only would improve my life, but would also impact the lives of those around me.

I joined a community of people who were also on a quest to find answers, a better way of living, and success personally and professionally. I quickly got to know everyone on The Call. I started to realize that I had so much work to do.

On the Wake Up Call, we read and discuss different self-motivational books. I was always an avid reader, but I never focused on books that would teach me how to think, become the best version of myself, and follow my gut.

Learning the material allowed me to see the world through a different lens. Have you ever heard, "You're living from the outside in; you must learn to live from the inside out?"

Well, what did that mean? It meant slowly learning how to navigate and adopt new principles and develop habits of responding instead of reacting. It meant being more patient and understanding. I was learning that circumstantial things always will be. How I choose to view things and the thoughts I frame around them would always be my choice. I started to see positivity and greatness around me.

As the community grew, these mornings were becoming not just habitual with repetition but rather a part of me, and my new way of living. I was learning that I needed to start shifting my focus, positivity, and what I wanted onto myself. "What do I want?" is not a question we ask ourselves.

I wore so many hats that I stopped asking myself what I wanted. By focusing on what I want, I move toward different goals. My mindset shifted to seeing everything through a lens of gratitude and opportunity.

After two years of study, mentorship, community sharing and learning, that voice inside calling me to do more and be more began surfacing as the voice God gave me, the one muted for years by the outside noise and everyday living. I could hear myself think and had come to an awakening after one of our community members shared an essay he wrote called I AM.

It would be the catalyst to push me forward on a new, unfamiliar, and comforting journey. Perhaps the countless ways I AM would show up in my life was the reassurance I needed to find someone greater than me. There are no coincidences. I AM showed up for me in many forms: a Lenten calendar, a suggested phone app, a movie my son needed help writing about in school, and the towels I ordered online branded I AM. The message was loud and clear; I would pursue my inner voice and what is meant for me.

A new beginning

In October 2021, after 17 years of corporate roles, I left my VP position and entered the world of entrepreneurship. I opened my company after tapping into what my true talents were, and would go on to help the network I'd built over the years. After a lengthy discovery of uncovering the meaning, "that I was meant for more," Rise Consulting and Communications was born. My morpho butterfly logo represents growth and evolution, and the name Rise is to help others rise to be their best in business. The vision was so clear.

I wasn't guessing anymore. I was on a new journey where I knew anything was possible, where abundance is meant for me after years of believing I deserved nothing. I wasn't going to feel like a yo-yo trying to figure out how to keep moving forward, when I was constantly being yanked back to a place of comfort and familiarity.

After so much study and discovery, I learned that growth lies in discomfort, and when we push ourselves the most to become comfortable with change, that is where we catapult to success.

I'm grateful for waking up in gratitude. I am part of something greater, a community of helping people, a coach, mentor, and friend. I'm enriched in ways I can't express.

Pep Talk

The I AM Essay was so impactful for so many of our members that it has been mentioned a few times in this book. Why was Silvio's essay so impactful? Michele quoted me saying, "The biggest problem we have in the world is ignorance." Although many believe that ignorance is bliss, I believe it's the root of all evil! It is the cause of our living in bondage. It's the cause of racism, ageism, and sexism. It's the cause of our treating symptoms and not causes. It's the cause of us not knowing who we are, and not knowing our capabilities. Ignorance will never be accepted as a valid defence in the court of man-made laws. In the same way, it will never be accepted by the universe to relieve you from suffering the effects of violating universal laws. We don't know what we don't know, which can cause us to feel stuck, drifting into some life we eventually come to question was meant for us. We have everything we need already inside of us, we just don't know it. Everything begins to change when we become aware of it!

The I AM essay gives people an awareness of who we are as creative beings. It reminds us of our ability to speak things into existence and moves us toward living a more intentional life!

"You can not escape a prison if you do not know you're in one"

—Vernon Howard.

What do you really want?

By Silvio Azzinnari

O n many occasions, Joe Trimboli would ask, "What do you want? What do you really want?" It was a question that I had heard often asked, however I had never actually taken the time to consider. Then one day that changed. It changed during a Wake Up Call. The group that morning was reading a statement followed by a question from a book written by Neale Donald Walsch.

"Do not let your life represent anything but the grandest version of the greatest vision you have ever had about who you are. Now, what is the most incredible vision you have ever had for yourself?"

This passage inspired me to ask myself, "What do I really want? What is the greatest vision I have for myself? What is the absolute grandest version of that vision?"

I sat back in my chair, closed my eyes, quieted my mind, and listened. Suddenly visions came into my mind's eye and a little voice whispered, "Share the stories you have inside of you."

For many years, I would envision stories and play with the idea of bringing my stories to life, however it would always end with the same old excuse. "One day, I will do it." That day never arrived, however the idea became real while sitting in that chair—write that story!

An overwhelming feeling

It was an overwhelming feeling, one that made me emotional. I instantly knew it was the right idea, and it became crystal clear what I wanted. I wanted to be a writer—an accomplished writer. It would have been great except for my self-image.

English has always been my worst subject. Every year I either failed English class or came close. I hated reading back then and it showed in my work. My spelling was horrible, my grammar terrible, and my handwriting horrendous. Moreover, my teachers let me know how bad I was doing in their classes.

I was raised with the idea that I was a terrible writer. That is who I was, according to my self-image. There was no idea that was further in my self-image, than the idea that I could be a writer. The possibility of becoming the next Prime Minister of Canada seemed more likely than the idea of me writing a book. But that overwhelming positive feeling I had while asking myself what I really wanted was leaving me with no doubt—I wanted to become a writer.

It seemed unlikely. This idea could have been one of many that came and went. However, luckily for me, I mentioned my experience during one Wake Up Call.

The community encouraged me to chase my dream. I could do whatever I wanted if I just believed in myself, I was told. And while I lacked faith in myself, their faith suddenly made it seem possible.

Soon after, an idea came to me—one that seemed very profound to me. Joe agreed that this was an idea that should be shared. He then reminded me that I had mentioned earlier that I wanted to be a writer, and that this idea could provide the perfect opportunity to write my first piece.

At first, I mockingly replied, "Yes, I should," but Joe reminded me of my dream and encouraged me to go after it. He lit a fire in me. And after giving it a moment of thought, I agreed, "Yes, this would be a perfect opportunity!"

And so, for the first time in over 30 years, I picked up a pen and wrote something that a teacher had not assigned. I did what a writer does—write!

I spent a few weeks pouring out all my thoughts onto paper. I read it, reread it, changed it, and edited it until it was finally ready. It was such an inspiring period. As I was writing, I recall my awareness shifting from time to time, and I would ask, "Who is writing this? It doesn't sound like the way I speak or write." It almost felt like an out-of-body experience. Yet, it was one of the most enjoyable moments of my life.

I shared my completed essay with Joe. After reading it, he insisted that I share it with the Wake Up Call community.

"What? Are you kidding?" was my response.

"There is no way I will do that! It is one thing to write privately, but to share it publicly, especially the first thing I ever wrote! No, that would not happen.", I stated.

But again, Joe had much greater faith in me than I had. He encouraged me to step outside my comfort zone, assuring me my essay would be well received. He believed that the message in the essay should be shared and that it would be selfish to keep it to myself. I trusted Joe, so I reluctantly agreed.

I AM

Finally the day to read my I AM essay arrived, and my doubts and fears crept in. That little voice inside saying, "Who am I to do this?" and, "What was I thinking when I agreed to do this?" was getting louder. But it was too late to back out. Trust me, if I could have, I would have.

The group was waiting to hear what I had written. So, with shaking hands and a trembling voice, I dove in, put my head down, and read my essay aloud.

I cannot overstate the response I received. It was moving and overwhelming. The community responded in a way that I will never forget. It was well-received and it did have a big impact on others. So much so, that many have reached out to me to share in their gratitude.

Much has happened to me since writing that piece, but there are too many to report here. Suffice it to say, many incredible people and experiences have come into my life, none more important than discovering how much I love to write.

The deep passion I now have for writing goes far beyond my realm of thinking before joining the call. With that passion buried deep in my childhood doubts and fears, my self-image would have never allowed the possibility that I could be a writer. I am forever grateful to the members of the Wake Up Call and to Joe, who offered me the platform to discover and share my passion. Without them, I may have never received my wake-up call.

Pep Talk

Our purpose is not something we go and find. It's something we uncover. It's something we already have within. Our purpose is something we love to do, would do all day, every day and not care if we ever got paid for it.

When you read Silvio's essay, you'll see that there's no question that writing "I AM" was the work of his higher self. In Marianne Williamson's poem *Our deepest fear*, she writes, "Your playing small does not serve the world." How often do we let our ego hold us back? We're concerned with how we will look and what people will think. Will people like us?

We all get that little spark that excites us, that idea that inspires us. It's too bad that most ideas are stillborn. These ideas are buried by wrong thinking—lies we've come to believe over time. Some of these lies could even be our grades in school or the teacher's opinions of our abilities. These lies make it impossible for these ideas to take on any kind of life. We don't act on them because of these distorted beliefs, and we deprive the world of its benefit.

You'll understand what I mean by this when you read I AM. After you read it, take a minute to let it sink in. See how Silvio's negative self-image could've stopped him from writing I AM, and you and I from benefiting from his message.

> *"It's not what you are that holds you back,*
> *it's what you think you're not."*
>
> — Dennis Waitley.

I AM — The two most powerful words ever spoken

By Silvio Azzinnari

I AM, two words that I have heard and said so many times in the past, but recently took on a very different meaning for myself.

I recently viewed a documentary, during which the host of the program was asking questions about God. During this dialogue, the host asked the following question. "Do you ever take God's name in vain?" The people would, in most cases, respond that they did not. The interviewer then proceeded to ask, "Do you ever say 'oh my God or OMG?'" Insinuating that every time that was said, they were indeed using God's name in vain. The people would be a bit surprised by this statement and then questioned themselves. Maybe they indeed had done something wrong or offended God by saying OMG.

When I heard this, something inside said, this can't be right. To be honest, ever since I was a child, I never understood this particular commandment. The explanations surrounding this commandment never felt right or complete to me. I could not accept that this was what God intended in the 3rd Commandment, "Thou shall not take The Lord God's Name in Vain." It was not in line with the idea of God that I held. I could not imagine, nor accept that our all-loving, all-forgiving Father would be so offended by people saying OMG, that it would require him to come down from on high to inscribe this into stone for generations to come. I felt that surely there must be more to this, that I am missing something here, that maybe something must have been lost in translation.

Then one day something occurred to me. All these names that we call God, such as Creator, Deity, Infinite Intelligence, Providence, Allah and Lord are names that we, as human beings, have named God. This is not what God referred to himself as. This is not the name God called himself.

In the book of Exodus, which appears in the Torah of the Jewish faith and the Old Testament of the Bible, God spoke to Moses on Mount Sinai next to the burning bush. At that time, He asks Moses to go to Egypt to help free the Israelites. Moses, questioning his ability to do such a thing and whether the Israelites would even believe him, asks God, "When I go to free them and tell them that The God of your ancestors has sent me, they will surely ask, 'what is his name?' and what shall I tell them?"

And in Exodus 3:14–15, God responds: "I AM THAT I AM, YOU WILL TELL THEM I AM HAS SENT YOU. THIS IS MY NAME FOREVER. THIS IS WHAT ALL FUTURE GENERATIONS ARE TO CALL ME."

It is in this answer to Moses' question that God tells us for the first time his name, and that name is I AM.

I decided to look at that 3rd Commandment again and replace the Lord God's name with the two words that God himself told us was his name, and from that came this…

"Thou shall not take the Lord God's name in vain" changed to, "Thou shall not take I AM in vain."

Now I had to ask, what is the definition of vain? I decided to look that up in dictionaries, and two very different definitions appeared. The first definition of vain was the one that was more familiar to me.

VAIN definition #1: having or showing an excessively high opinion of one's appearance, abilities, or worth.

Used in a sentence: "His flattery made him vain."

Similar words: conceited, narcissistic.

The second definition of vain I found a little bit more interesting.

VAIN definition #2: producing no result; useless.

Used in a sentence: "A vain attempt to tidy up the room" or, "They tried in vain".

Similar Words: unsuccessful, producing wrong results, undesired result (what you don't want) or missing the mark, (which is said to be the word SIN in Hebrew text translated into the English language).

With this new clarity on the definition of vain, I once again turned to the 3rd Commandment:

"Thou shall not take the Lord God's name in Vain," literally translates to,

Thou shall not use I AM for what you don't want.

That bears repeating.

Thou shall not use I AM for what you don't want.

This hit me hard and caused me to pause, but it immediately felt right.

For it is when we say I am weak, I am unworthy, I am unloved, and I am less than, that we are in fact taking the Lord God's name in vain. It is when we use God's name or I AM for what we don't want that we are doing precisely what the 3rd commandment is warning us not to do. It is why we are told in Joel 3:10, "Let the weak man say, I AM strong." We are being shown how to use God's name correctly as a statement or declaration for what we do want. It is not saying that you won't be weak, that you won't struggle or experience what you don't want, but despite that, you have the power to change it, to create what you do want. And you do that by invoking God's name correctly, by saying, I AM STRONG!

I AM, is a state of being-ness. It is who you are being in this everlasting moment of now. In these two words, you are declaring who you are and who you declare yourself to be and hold in a state of faith or belief, which will be exactly what you create or attract into your experience.

Who we currently are, is a result of all the little I AM's we have picked up along the way in this journey we call life. It is all these I AM's that we have accepted and therefore consented to, and believed to be true for ourselves, that is creating the life experience we are all living. Many, if not most of these I AM's we inherited from others: our parents, teachers and peers, and as such we unknowingly have agreed to them without giving them any thought. Therefore we have accepted these declarations, not of our own volition but by someone else's.

Therefore seek not to blame the circumstance, the person, or the situations for your current reality, for in truth, it was in your declaration of Who You Are or Who I AM in relation to that event that your reality was formed. In other words, things happen—it just is what it is, but what you are saying about that occurrence, is the experience you are creating for yourself. Are we declaring I AM a victim? I AM less than or I AM unworthy or some other thought that does not serve us? Or are we choosing to declare I AM a child of the most high God, I AM worthy or I AM strong. Therefore, if a current I AM no longer serves you, choose again and then choose again. For it is in the choosing and re-choosing of who I AM that lies in our power to create.

And create you will do, in fact it is all we can do. We are made in the image and likeness of God and God is a creator. We are creating all the time because we are creative beings. We have been told that we are here to do God's work and what is God's work? It is to create—that is what a creator does. We are constantly creating with our thoughts, words and deeds or in other words, we create by what we think, what we say and what we do. These are our paintbrushes on the canvas of our lives, so to speak. All of these are statements of I AM.

The Law of Polarity or The Law of Opposites decrees that everything has an equal and opposite side, so it is not just in what we think, but also in what we do not think. It is in what we say and also in what we do not say. In what we do and in what we do not do, we are also declaring our I AM's. It is always the thought, behind the thought, behind the thought, that your true declarations of who you are exist, or the I AM's that you have believed, accepted, and hold to be true for you.

There is but one statement we make in life and that is a continual expression of our I AM's. Whatever follows I AM is your reality. Your belief and ongoing declarations of this belief through what you think, say and do, make this so.

With this new understanding, it helps some other biblical quotes make sense for me. I believe it is why we are told, "whatever you ask for in my name (I AM), it will be given unto you" and, "to call forth those things that do not exist as if they did" and you do that by invoking the most powerful two words ever spoken—I AM.

> *"For by your words will you be justified and*
> *by your words will you be condemned."*
> — Matthew 12:37.

About the Author

Joe is a Mortgage Broker, author, entrepreneur, mindset coach, speaker and founder of the Wake Up Call™ and Pep Talks™.

Although Joe has achieved some impressive results in both his mortgage and coaching business, he's not about the bling and doesn't flaunt his success. He understands that achieving goals is not about getting the material things, achieving goals is about the growth necessary to becoming the person that is capable of achieving those goals.

Joe is obsessed with sharing what he's learned and gets his reward from helping other people create the life they dream of, and loves celebrating their wins along with them.

He spent the first 40 years of his life in the dark and as he started to become aware of the real meaning of a positive mindset and how to apply it, saw his results drastically improve. He dedicated himself to sharing what he's learned with people so they can develop the confidence and unwavering faith necessary to achieve anything they set their minds to, but more importantly because he has learned, firsthand, that people don't need to be struggling the way they do.

Joe has appeared on several podcasts, delivered inspiring talks to corporations like Saks 5th Avenue, First National, The Mortgage Centre, Mortgage Architects, Re/Max, Royal LePage, Simplicity Car Care, to name a few, and has coached stay-at-home moms, lawyers, presidents, CEOs, salespeople, employees, students, young people and old. He runs his own workshops and hosts a daily call where he leads members from all over the world in the study of the most influential and powerful books ever written.

Many of his members and listeners have credited him for their life-changing results, and a variety of different achievements, but the one thing almost all of them had in common, is they gained peace of mind.

www.joetrimboli.com

CONTINUE YOUR JOURNEY WITH US

Scan the QR code or visit www.joetrimboli.com and Register to join the Wake Up Call™!

Enter **YOURWAKEUPCALL** at checkout to receive a FREE One-Month Membership as our gift to you!

I'm ready for my Wake Up Call!

SCAN ME

#VIBRATEHIGHER

Acknowledgements

Thank you, dad, for always encouraging me to think. To never stand around with my hands in my pockets and to never follow the crowd.

Thank you, mama, for showing me kindness. For teaching me to find the good in things and to always go above and beyond. You give everything you have and never expect anything in return. You taught me by doing, not by preaching, and I love you for that. I wish you peace in your heart always.

Thank you, Bob Proctor, my mentor. I wouldn't be where I am today if it weren't for your teachings, and neither would any members of the Wake Up Call or the readers of this book. "Bob, not only will I equal your achievements in life, but I am going to challenge you at the post and pass you at the grandstand." Rest well, knowing that although your body has left us, you continue to teach us every day and continue to change the lives of millions all over the world.

Thank you to the founding members, Dave Palazzese, Rich Spence and Mike Verrelli. You guys were showing up on mornings when I wasn't and encouraged me to keep on this path. You were the environment I needed to grow in, while I was just a little seedling. We're the original four and I wouldn't have it any other way!

Thank you, Silvio Azzinnari. Your perspective allowed me to see things in a new light and got me going in the right direction. I AM has already changed so many lives and I'm humbled to have witnessed you step into your purpose and honoured to feature your essay in this book.

Thank you to all the members of the Wake Up Call™. Because of you, we have created the perfect environment for so many people to grow and thrive. It fills my heart to see the friendships that have formed and the connection among you. I'm so grateful for this community.

Thank you to my very own "Ginas", Claudia and Lori. Your support, dedication and loyalty allow me to show up in ways I couldn't if not for you two running the show! You've allowed me to focus on what I want, and because of you I'm doing what I love every day!

My big sister, Vivi (Elvira). Having you on the calls has made the early zoom calls feel a little more like home. Your bravery, commitment, loyalty, and kindness have inspired me and so many others, in ways that you don't even know.

Thank you, Rita, for giving me the space in our home to grow. I do my work knowing that I have your support. I couldn't be as passionate as I am at 5 a.m. if I were not allowed to go into "Full Moon Joe" mode first thing in the morning.

To my girls, Sofia, Ava, and Erica. You are the reason I woke up. Without you, there'd be no inspiration for my life. I can only hope and pray that you will come to live by some of these lessons that daddy learned the hard way. I hope you don't inherit too much of what I couldn't "fix", but I know you have everything you need to fix what I didn't. I look at each one of you with a full heart and know that you will come to know how incredibly powerful you are. Be kind, dream big and believe you can do anything— because you can! I'm so incredibly proud of each of you. May the right words you hear from me take root in your heart and propel you toward a full and happy life, while the wrong words fall away and disintegrate into nothingness.

Thank you, God. If anyone is suffering, it's only because they don't know the laws that work so perfectly, for everyone, every time. You've always been there, even when I wasn't listening. You've always believed in me. Always guided me. Always gave me the air that I need to breathe. This magic lives in all of us and I'm grateful to have experienced it for myself. This is the greatest love on earth. With you, I can create!

Thank you to all the contributing authors. It takes courage to be vulnerable and share your stories. Each one of you has inspired me and I know your stories will give so many people the Wake Up Call they need. This collaboration has been an amazing example of the magic that happens when you make a decision, and then figure out "how" to do it, only after the decision has been made. Congratulations to each of you. Thank you for helping me tell the world that, "if I can do it, anyone can."

Thank you Brian Proctor. One of my favourite things you shared with us is how you and your dad would speak on the phone every morning and "talk good about people behind their back". Well, you should know that people are in the habit of talking good about you behind your back. One of my favourite quotes is from Matthew 23:13: "he who humbles himself will be exalted." I, as many others do, hold you in the highest regard and am honoured to have you write the foreword of this book. I can only imagine how much you miss those calls with Bob but hope you'll feel better knowing the ripple effect of having shared them with us!